INSIDE GREEK TERRORISM

GEORGE KASSIMERIS

Inside Greek Terrorism

HURST & COMPANY, LONDON

First published in the United Kingdom in paperback in 2013 by
C. Hurst & Co. (Publishers) Ltd.,
41 Great Russell Street, London, WC1B 3PL

Printed in India

A Cataloguing-in-Publication data record for this book is available from the British Library.

ISBN: 9781849042833

www.hurstpublishers.com

This book is printed on paper from registered sustainable and managed sources.

For you, Carolina Salinas

CONTENTS

ACKNOWLEDGMENTS

The greatest pleasure at the completion of a book is to thank publicly those who have contributed directly or indirectly, in a major or minor way, to its creation. My first debt—and it is a very large one—is to the Leverhulme Trust, for awarding me a generous Research Fellowship, and to the Nuffield Foundation and the British Academy for funding different stages of the research on which this book is based. Without the financial support of these great British institutions, this project might not have taken off the ground.

My second debt, equally large, is to Dimitris and Evgenia Afendoulis for their forbearance, support and the truly extraordinary constancy of their hospitality.

I am deeply grateful once again to my best friend, mentor and editor, Carol Millwood, for her penetrating criticism, advice and her unfailing support, especially at times of extreme pressure. This is the fourth book we have done together, and I cannot imagine this process without her. Richard Jackson and Marie Breen Smyth, friends, colleagues and fellow editors at the *Critical Studies on Terrorism* journal, offered me support, ideas and encouragement from the very earliest stages of the project. I would also like to record my warmest gratitude to Ignacio Sanchez-Cuenca and Peter Neumann who were extremely supportive from the beginning. A series of long, fascinating conversations with Richard Bond and Peppe Egger helped me to formulate some of the arguments and ideas on which the book is based. I would also like to thank Bruce Hoffman who enthusiastically supported and promoted this project from the outset.

The University of Wolverhampton was consistently supportive of the project and provided an excellent setting for thinking and writing. My thanks are due to my colleagues in the Politics, History and War Studies Department for their support, in particular, John Buckley, Paul Henderson and the Dean of School, Judith Burnett.

Among the many individuals who have shared with me their specialist knowledge and advice, for which I very grateful, are Fiona Andrikopoulou, Sylla Alexiou, Crispin Black, Martha Crenshaw, Dimitris Dimopoulos, Frank Faulkner, Andreas Gofas, Dipak Gupta, Benoit Gomis, Lee Jarvis, Brady Kiesling, Costas Kyriakopoulos, Rania Karabliani, Elena Lazarou, Diego Muro, Mina Moustaka, Huma Mumtaz, Michalis Margaritis, Maria Margaronis, Dennis Pluchinsky, Nina-Maria Paschalidou, Jason Ralph, Simon Reid-Henry, Wyn Rees, Panagiotis Roumeliotis, Robert Saunders, Diane Shugart, Caroline Soper, Bob Spencer, Tim Naftali, Mark Tuley and Nikolaos Zairis.

Finally, I am grateful to the Hurst and Oxford University Press peer-reviewers for their feedback and valuable suggestions. One suggestion was the addition of a post-introduction contextual chapter that provides a historical overview of the ideological evolution of Greek terrorism. Some of the ideas and material in Chapter 2 have developed out of earlier work that I did in my book *Europe's Last Red Terrorists: The Revolutionary Organization 17 November* published by Hurst and New York University Press. I should also note that some of the material in the book appeared initially in *Terrorism and Political Violence*, *Studies in Conflict & Terrorism* and *International Affairs* and I thank the publishers and editors of these journals for permission to use it here.

AUTHOR'S BIOGRAPHY

George Kassimeris is Reader in Terrorism Studies at the University of Wolverhampton, UK and is author/editor of six books including, *Europe's Last Red Terrorists*; *The Barbarization of Warfare* and *Playing Politics with Terrorism: A User's Guide*.

1

INTRODUCTION

> While nothing is easier than to denounce the evildoer, nothing is more difficult than to understand him
>
> Fyodor Dostoevsky

It was at 10:25 on Saturday 29 June 2002 when the extraordinarily long run of luck of Europe's most elusive terrorist group, the Revolutionary Organization 17 November (17N), finally ran out. A strong blast ripped through the warm evening air near the ticket office of Hellas Flying Dolphins in the port of Piraeus. One man was seriously injured in the face, hands and chest. It seemed that the bomb he was carrying, concocted from alarm clocks, common detonators, 9-volt batteries and dynamite had gone off prematurely. Port authorities rushed to the scene and the man was taken to the emergency unit of the nearby Tzanneio hospital.

Early reports speculated that the bomber was a member of one of the country's smaller terrorist groups such as the Revolutionary Cells or Popular Resistance which had been relatively active. But the contents of a rucksack (a .38 handgun and two hand grenades) found near to the injured man, soon identified as Savvas Xiros, proved much more tantalizing. Three days later, Police Chief Fotis Nassiakos announced that the .38 Smith and Wesson had been identified as the gun stolen from a police officer killed by 17N on the Christmas eve of 1984 and was the same weapon subsequently used in the assassinations of shipowner Costas Peratikos and prosecutor Costas Androulidakis as well as a number of other incidents involving the group. A member of the terrorist organization, often referred to as *organossi phantasma* or phantom organization, which had acted with impunity for twenty-seven years, was suddenly in police custody.

Xiros's arrest marked the beginning of the end for 17N. From his hospital bed and apparently fearing for his life, the icon painter and—as it turned out—a senior 17N gunman gave the prosecutor in charge of the anti-terrorism investigation critical information that fuelled a chain reaction of arrests that led to the dismantling of the group in less than a month.[1]

The final nail in 17N's coffin came on 5 September 2002 when the group's leader of operations, Dimitris Koufodinas, turned himself in to the police after two months on the run. Koufodinas pulled up at police headquarters on Alexandras Avenue in a taxi at 2:35 a.m., dressed in jeans, a black T-shirt, sunglasses and a jockey cap. 'I am Dimitris Koufodinas and I have come to turn myself in', he told the duty officer before being taken to the twelfth floor of the anti-terrorism squad. Koufodinas had been on the run since the 29 June premature detonation of the bomb Xiros was carrying in Piraeus. Xiros later told anti-terrorism officers that he had urged Koufodinas to flee the scene. Koufodinas, who had more than twenty-four hours to get away before police realized that Xiros was tied to 17N, ran first to one of the gang's hideouts in Pangrati where, according to Greek anti-terrorism sources, he destroyed evidence before going on the run. Unlike Alexandros Giotopoulos,[2] the group's chief ideologue who denied any involvement in 17N, Koufodinas went on to take full responsibility for the entire 17N experience and sought to defend the group's campaign from beginning to end.

In December 2003, after a marathon nine-month trial (the longest in modern Greek history) held in a purpose-built courtroom in Athens' largest maximum-security prison in Korydallos, a three-member tribunal convicted fifteen members of the group while another four defendants were acquitted due to a lack of sufficient evidence. The court upheld the state prosecutor's recommendation for twenty-one life terms and a twenty-five-year sentence for the alleged leader and chief ideologue while the group's operational leader, Koufodinas, received thirteen life sentences and twenty-five years in jail.[3]

The capture and imprisonment of Koufodinas, Giotopoulos and their group marked the demise of the last and most stubborn of a generation of ideological terrorists whose campaign caused serious political and security problems in Western Europe for more than a quarter of a century. However, in spite of the testimonies of more than 500 people and more than 900 hours of court hearings, the history of the foundation of the group remained unclear.[4] Given the sheer longevity of the entire 17N terrorist experience, one of the central objectives of this project is to analyse the life histories of imprisoned members of the defunct 17N group in order to answer three particularly intriguing and related questions: 'Who were these people?', 'Where did they come from?' and, more crucially, 'What kept them inside the terrorist organization for so long?'

Studies of Europe's most enduring ideological terrorist groups have shown that organizations relied heavily for their long-term strength and survival on the existence of a clear moral identity characterized by solidarity, strong emotional bonds and a quasi-religious devotion to an ideological cause.[5] In the case of 17N, three of the terrorists were brothers, two were cousins and one was godfather to the other's children. In other words, blood bonds, so important in Greek society, reinforced trust and silence, helping to explain the group's operational continuity and remarkable resistance to infiltration. At the same time, however, the fact that 17N's members were so few and so close to each other also meant that once its structure cracked it crumbled like a 'house of cards', to use the phrase of veteran US State Department terrorism analyst Dennis Pluchinsky,[6] which is exactly what happened on 29 June 2002 with the premature detonation of the bomb Xiros was carrying in Piraeus.

In the case of armed groups such as the Italian Red Brigades (BR) or the German Red Army Faction (RAF), telling the life stories of three or four members would probably be insufficient to understand what led the groups to behave as they did, mainly because the organizations consisted of considerably more than a handful of adherents. But in the case of 17N, comparatively a very small group with a more defined rank-and-file structure, such an approach could work. Analyzing the life histories of former members of 17N, such as Koufodinas and Patroklos Tselentis, offers valuable insights into the development of complex processes of involvement in and disengagement from terrorism. The detail stemming from the life stories of former militants provides a more complete picture of the group's internal dynamics and challenges a range of simplistic stereotypes, not only about the individuals involved in terrorism but also about the ways in which they made decisions and reflected on their experiences of being part of a terrorist organization. This research will confirm that there is no single route to terrorism nor single route away from it. The biographies of the Greek militants indicate that involvement in terrorist activity, and subsequent exit from a terrorist organization, is experienced differently by individuals even when it concerns members of the same organization.

There has been a great deal of scholarship on why individuals or groups resort to terrorism but there has been comparatively little analysis of why individual terrorists end their involvement in violent activities.[7] Given the potential value of such analysis for counterterrorism efforts, understanding individual exit from a terrorist organization should be viewed as having the same urgency as examining the reasons why people join such organizations and why they choose to remain in them.

As such, a further objective in analyzing the life histories of imprisoned members of the defunct Revolutionary Organization 17 November was to look for causes of disengagement, dissociation and repentance. Through analysis of key primary source material and through conducting a broad range of interviews with former group members, their legal teams, close associates of the jailed and released militants, as well as key members of the police and security services and criminal justice professionals, who have interacted with the terrorists and therefore have genuine insights into their personalities, the author was able to determine some of the factors and motivations pushing individuals into giving up terrorist violence. The research aimed to collect data from interviews with former members of the group in order to understand why they left, what factors were prevalent at various points in the process that precipitated their exit, and what the exiting process and experience of life as an ex-terrorist was like.

Conducting interviews, however, with imprisoned members of the 17N group proved extremely challenging. In order to gain access to 17N members the author had to go through their defence lawyers, and that proved a time-consuming and, at times, awkward process as there was a certain degree of mistrust on the part of the militants' legal teams. Some 17N defence lawyers in particular tended to also act as their clients' spokesmen, middle-men (or middle-women as was the case for Koufodinas's lawyer) and media and image advisors. In the case of Koufodinas, for example, an interview would be only be granted, if the author was prepared and willing to submit his text comprising the interview material prior to publication for authorization and approval.[8] Needless to say the interview never took place when it was explained that the role of the academic researcher was to not to help embellish a certain image Koufodinas's legal team might have wanted him to portray in public but to collect, interpret and analyze information independently. In another case, a 17N militant was willing to talk to the author only to suddenly withdraw from the process a few interviews later on the grounds that my research would 'help the forces of counter-terrorism'. Another militant gave his time generously and spoke freely about past events but when he discovered that there would in all probability be a Greek edition of this book, asked the author to withhold his name, which served as a further reminder, if not confirmation, of the complex, paranoid and dark underside of Greek radical politics. Given the volatility of the subject matters and after taking legal advice, a decision was made not to source any of these interviews and to keep the names of all other interviewees (involved in terrorism) anonymous in the text.

The situation was made even more difficult because the field work coincided with a change of government in Greece and in Greek political discourse, which always results in a complete change of top personnel in key positions at the Ministries of Justice and Public Order as well as the police and security services. At the same time, requests to conduct interviews in a prison environment were refused by the prison authorities on the basis that only first-degree relatives and defence lawyers were allowed access to the prisoners. In the end, after considerable time was spent in establishing rapport with the defence lawyers and family members, the author was able to conduct a number of interviews with prisoners on the phone.

While initially this appeared to be far from ideal, it progressively became clear that for the interviewees this type of interviewing provided an 'objective' setting in which they could relive some of their experiences. There were a number of specific themes the author pursued and explored with each interviewee, although the sequence in which they were introduced was unstructured and determined primarily by the mood of the interviewee, which varied from interview to interview. Interviewees could be angry, acute, open, self-pitying, sarcastic, absolutist, emotional and defensive. The author quickly came to realize, during the course of the research, that the effects of long-term imprisonment and the emotional state and fragility of the interviewee were to determine the flow of the interview and the issues discussed.[9]

One characteristic case was Xiros. There can be no question that he was the man whose hospital testimony led to the arrest of most of his comrades and formed the cornerstone of the Greek state's case against 17N. Claiming repeatedly that he was forced by the anti-terrorism authorities to give names and denounce the terrorist group he once served, Xiros became something of a tragic figure in the 17N story. His tragedy stemmed from his inability (or even refusal) to come to terms with his guilt for what happened and it has been the tension between guilt and reality that have run through Xiros's existence ever since Koufodinas decided to surrender. From the moment Xiros found himself reunited with 17N's operational leader inside Korydallos prison, he tried to exorcise, if not delete, the reality of his previous actions with contradictory statements and rants about plots, threats and psychotropic medicines.[10]

Marinos Pittaridis, the doctor who looked after Xiros at Evagellismos Hospital and saved his life, saw things differently. This is how he described to me the whole episode and he is worth quoting in full:

> The security inside but also outside the hospital was unprecedented. Surrounded by police the hospital felt more like a high-security prison than a public hospital. Every day we had to go through countless checks. Our name, our position in the hospital, our daily tasks were checked. What time we went in, what time we left. The truth is that it took a while for the doctors and staff to win the trust of the anti-terrorist squad officers. In their eyes, those first days, we were all suspect terrorists.
>
> When Savvas Xiros was brought into the intensive care unit, we did not know what type of terrorist he was, meaning what terrorist group was he from. We were kept in the dark. Until we learned from TV who Savvas Xiros was, we never imagined that he could be a 17 November member. As a doctor I felt a huge responsibility in making sure that everything that could be done to save him was done. I'm pretty sure that if Xiros hadn't made it, there would be plenty of people out there accusing us of not trying hard enough.
>
> When you do a job like mine, the first thing you need to have is neutrality. You must never confuse emotions and duty. Never discriminate. From the very first moment, I tried to push away the thought that the patient in that intensive care unit was a terrorist who had spread death. For me he was just another patient who you have to try to keep alive. Savvas Xiros has tried to make excuses to his comrades for what happened but the truth is that he and only he wanted to talk. And he didn't talk because we gave

> him medication that makes you talk—such medication doesn't exist anyway—but because he was really scared that they would come after him and kill him. I remember trying to calm him down telling him not to worry, that it's all over and him saying to me: is it really, or is this the beginning? When he began talking to the anti-terrorism prosecutor and the chief of the anti-terrorism squad, he would talk non-stop till the early hours of the morning. I asked him several times if he wanted me to intervene so he wouldn't have to talk for so long but every time I asked him, he would say: No. Let me talk; let me get it out of the way.[11]

The collapse of 17N was not the end of the story for Greek terrorism. It is probably not unfair to state that at the time a considerable number of senior officials at the Greek Ministry of Public Order that the author spoke to seriously entertained the theory that 17N's dismantling was equivalent to the final elimination of terrorism in Greece, insisting that any remaining small stubborn splinter groups posed no real security threat. If only it were that simple, for European experience has repeatedly shown that when a major terrorist organization is broken, after a period of time a new generation of terrorists emerges. This new generation may lack the operational capabilities and scope of the group they aspire to imitate but that does not render them less dangerous. Tellingly, in the Greek context, a new group calling itself Revolutionary Struggle (RS) first picked up the baton of violence from 17N before the latter's trial had even come to an end. RS was joined in 2008 by a second anarchist-oriented guerrilla group, the Conspiracy of Cells of Fire (CCF), which went on to become the most active of Greece's new generation of urban guerrilla groups. Another important focus of this book has been to examine the campaigns of violence of this new generation of urban guerrilla groups and explain their strategy, tactical focus and selection of targets as well as the nature of their organizational and operational development. In consequence it will place the post-17N rise in Greek extremism and violence in a broader political and cultural perspective, and define what these new terrorist groups seek to achieve, what motivates their actions and how they compare with their predecessors.

2

GREEK POLITICAL VIOLENCE IN CONTEXT

Revolutionary behaviour cannot be studied apart from its sociopolitical and ideological environment. Revolutionary terrorism in Greece resulted from a complex series of political conditions and long-standing cultural influences that drew politically active individuals towards the utopian world of revolutionary protest and violence. These conditions and influences provided the foundations upon which extreme-left terrorism took firm root in the mid-1970s and must be analysed in greater depth and placed within the wider context of the evolution of the Greek political culture within the last forty years, especially the years following the collapse the Colonels' dictatorial regime in 1974. Within this primarily contemporary political context, the focus is more specifically on the origins and characteristics of violence and the extent and intensity of violent protest to the political establishment, and less on a wide-ranging contemporary historical narrative of national events and developments.

The Postwar Period

Political violence has not been a stranger to the history, culture and institutions of modern Greece. By the end of 1974, Greeks have had a taste of all political situations: a bitter taste on the whole. From the end of the Second World War to the early 1970s, the country suffered in quick succession Nazi occupation, a senseless and catastrophic civil war, a period of quasi-parliamentary rule of low legitimacy with strong police and autocratic characteristics, and finally a harsh military dictatorship.

The civil war (1946–49) between communists and anti-communists, in which over 80,000 Greeks were killed and 700,000 lost their homes, not only generated a passionate and profound political division within a country already devastated by the ravages of the Second World War and the brutal German occupation but it was also to cast, through its fanaticism and ferocity, a long shadow over the politics of the 1950s and 1960s. The deep political and social wounds inflicted upon the national psyche even to this day have not yet fully healed.

The institutional legacy of the civil war survived until 1974, largely the systematic discrimination by the victors (the Right) against the vanquished (the Left). Discrimination against the vanquished of the civil war was enforced through what became known as the 'paraconstitution', a draconian set of emergency laws modelled on US anti-communist legislation, and political control techniques, used extensively during the Truman-McCarthy era, aiming for the political and economic exclusion of the Greek left and the consolidation of the anti-communist state.[1] Anti-communism bolstered authoritarianism everywhere: in the civil service, the armed forces, the police and the universities. Dissent and any form of politico-ideological criticism were banned and there was a complete absence of any 'grouping, newspaper or periodical advocating a non-communist alternative to reaction in the political, social and cultural sphere'.[2]

Discrimination and political and economic exclusion were imposed by a large police bureaucracy which kept files on every Greek citizen. With red ink police would underline critical information about citizens or their relatives labelled as communists or leftist sympathizers. The police files and the police-issued civic-mindedness certificates implemented a brand of totalitarianism which involved collective family responsibility and mass political surveillance through police informers who numbered over 60,000 by the early 1960s.[3] A series of special paraconstitutional legislations (laws 509/1947 and 516/1948 in particular), which operated alongside and in flagrant violation of the Greek constitution, enabled the security police to terrorize, persecute and ostracize citizens of 'doubtful' political morality.[4] By the end of the 1950s, an 'impenetrable ideological and political ghetto'[5] was firmly in place, with anti-communism 'turning from an instrument of state legislation to the governing principle of an aggressive strategy of social demobilization and of social control designed to safeguard the closed nature of the Greek political system, reinforce it and above all to ensure its perpetuation'.[6]

Until the fall of the Colonels' regime in 1974 Greek citizens were pigeonholed into *ethnikofrones* ('healthy', nationally-minded) and *non-ethnikofrones* (communists and sympathizers). Such ideological divisions were to have, somewhat inevitably, serious side-effects on the evolution of Greek political culture within which extreme-left terrorism later emerged. Greece's post-civil war mechanisms of political control came under strain only once in the mid-1960s with the election victory of George Papandreou's Centre Union progressive party in November 1963 and again in February 1964. The Papandreou victories, together with the growing popular discontent over urban unemployment, income inequalities, poor access to higher education and a manipulative electoral system that disenfranchised a large minority, were evidence that the exclusivist parliamentary system could no longer survive without radical changes.[7] Such radical changes, however, were bound to deeply affect the main institutional pillars of the post-war political system (the throne-parliament-army triarchy in which the military was the dominant force) and to fundamentally alter the distribution of power among them. The Greek political system was confronted with a straightforward dilemma:

> either parliament, through its opening up to the masses, had to become the dominant force in this triarchy, in which case the army would lose its leading position with inevitable internal consequences for holding posts within it; or else the army had to prevent this by the overall abolition of parliamentary rule.[8]

The 'Revolution' of 21 April 1967 was therefore an anxious attempt by an apprehensive military to preserve its supremacy. Committed to the perpetuation of the divisive ideology of the civil war, the armed forces abandoned their post-war role as mere arbitrators to parliamentary squabbles and forcibly seized a dominant role within the power structure in order to reorganize the country's political life by 'clearing the mess' and putting an end to the conditions of 'anarchy and chaos'[9] to which the political class (the Right and the King) had reduced Greece.[10] Although the army had intervened at different times in the past (1909, 1916 and 1922), it had never before questioned parliamentary rule, nor hat it sought to permanently replace civilian and parliamentary institutions. Until 1967, military interventions were 'essentially restricted to a moderator pattern' as they either advanced interests of specific political parties or sought to punish the entire political class for its failings.[11]

The Colonels' image as simple patriots crusading against communism, their loud commitment to the principles of Hellenism and orthodox Christianity and their populist rhetoric of spurious egalitarianism did not succeed in concealing the regime's fragility, anachronistic views and essential political weaknesses.[12] Despite this, the military junta managed to stay in power for seven years through political repression and with the help of an unprecedented international boom. Sporadic and uncoordinated resistance together with the resignation of a large section of a deeply disillusioned populace with parliamentary politics also fed a belief that the Colonels were better than the available alternatives.[13] At the same time, until the 1972–3 world oil crisis, rapid growth raised living standards and reduced any potential for meaningful protest. When the economic crisis did arrive it quickly drained confidence in the regime which appeared to be floundering in problems beyond its competence. The events of November 1973 and the brutal military suppression of the student occupation of the Athens Polytechnic turned public opinion against the regime and activated popular resistance, cementing the impression that political transformation might be possible.[14] In the end, the Colonels' junta dissolved when, in the summer of 1974, in a last-ditch attempt to regain domestic support through the manipulation of nationalist sentiment, it failed to influence events in Cyprus, losing the northern part of the island to Turkey.[15] At a deeper level, the Colonels' regime fell apart because it failed to overcome the problem which historically haunts most authoritarian models of government, namely 'the establishment of a political system with an appearance of a legitimacy that could succeed the dictatorship'.[16]

November 1973

Greece's repressive post-civil war socio-political system came almost to a halt in 1973 when national and international events taking place that year fuelled a belief among Greek university student activists that a direct confrontation with the military unta might after all be possible. The French *événements de mai* and the Italian *Il Sessantotto* and the Vietnamese victories against the US, exercised a powerful ideological influence on an increasingly restless university population.[17] The Vietnam war in particular had validated that 'a people, however weak, when they have belief in themselves and follow the correct revolutionary strategy, can even defeat a superpower'.[18] At the same time, protest demonstrations against the Greek junta in several European capitals further exposed public apathy. The regime, in a desperate attempt to pre-empt a generalized explosion, rushed through a number of educational and economic reforms but this failed to placate university activists and the workers. A series of national strikes and student demonstrations increased tension. The occupation of Athens University Law School in March[19] and Athens Polytechnic in November 1973 provoked a major crisis to the apparatus by igniting an apparent revolution. The Polytechnic events, in particular, became the epicentre of student dissent and served as an effective focus of opposition to the regime. Lasting a mere three days (14–17 November), the revolt not only challenged the military regime but catalysed popular mobilization in many sectors of Greek society. What had begun as a student protest against an authoritarian educational system escalated rapidly into a general political uprising against the military dictatorship.[20] Demanding '*Bread, Education and Liberty*' (the slogan of November 1973), the students provided anti-authoritarian ideology to a weak and pathetically resigned populace and unsettled an impending deal between the conservative old-right and the military on 'a stratocratic liberalization' based on the Chilean and Turkish models.[21]

Between 1969 and 1973 the number of university students rose significantly. In 1969 there were 12,175 new entrants, in 1972, 14,218 and in 1973, 15,389 out of a total 123,081 students congesting the universities of Athens and Salonika.[22] Moreover, the expansion of student numbers was not accompanied by the necessary expansion of lecture rooms or hire of extra full-time professors. During the 1970s, the number of full-time professors increased less than two-fold resulting to 'the worst student-teacher ratio in Europe'[23] (90:1 for the main teaching staff).[24] In short, this new generation of students entered a university system which was in an advanced state of malfunction. Student meetings, strikes and demonstrations about the quality and organization of studies, the lack of dialogue between teachers and students, the petty regulations in the student hostels, the nature of the teaching and the content of the courses, the lack of laboratories, the inadequate welfare services and the links between university bureaucracy and the military regime were met with arrests and police violence leading to wider and more radical protests.

Economic recession and rising unemployment further polarized attitudes. By November 1973, the number of jobless young people had risen to 200,000.[25] As recession deepened and job competition increased, students came to accept that unemployment was not an ephemeral phase but the next step after university graduation. This sense of insecurity and social marginalization prompted highly politicized students with Trotskyist and Maoist affiliations to 'construct a critique of society, the role of family and the values and content of the education system itself'.[26] External factors also contributed to shaping such attitudes. Despite the fact that the ideas of May 1968 did not reach Greece until 1971, it nonetheless 'brought to the surface not only the need for an incessant criticism of the old world, but also the urgency to prevent that need from being applied in a formalistic and impassable way. It questioned the economist and dogmatic hyperpolitical way of viewing things, and with its theoretical, political and social weight, shifted the centre of the debate'.[27] Losing credibility fast and confronted with a massive budgetary crisis, the military junta sought to liberalize the system and preserve it at the same time. Many political prisoners in exile were allowed to return.[28] The limits of permissible debate in the media and political forums were extended. Censorship was relaxed and this 'created a positive political and cultural climate that allowed comfortable margins for the pluralistic circulation of ideas'.[29] Publishers produced scores of new titles of all ideological trends and magazines devoted large amounts of space to Vietnam, the cultural revolution, the Sino-Soviet split, the death of Guevara, and the 1968 protest movements in France and Italy. Large sections of youth were 'brought into contact with the most significant works of historical and contemporary Marxist, anarchist, and bourgeois radical thought'.[30]

Student agitation began over long-standing, unresolved issues. Initial demands were for greater student participation in university and faculty governance, the democratization and modernization of the educational system and the abolition of legislation that restricted academic freedom. More specifically, the regime had instituted a commissar system under which they appointed retired or former military officers with wide powers of veto to 'supervise education and to see that every action of the university was in accord with the dictates of the government'.[31] It had also introduced in 1969 laws 93 and 180 which made provisions for harsh penalties for disciplinary offences and gave the commissioners 'the right to sit on all student meetings to guard over "national security interests"'.[32] As the liberalization experiment ran amok the junta quickly returned to its old repressive ways invoking special laws that gave the regime the power to 'revoke the deferment of students from national service because of wilful abstention from attendance at lectures and classes'.[33] From then onwards, as one demontsration followed another, protests against student conditions would swiftly turn into mass actions against the oppressive and authoritarian character of the regime, resulting in savage student-police battles which exposed the regime's barbarism and encouraged extreme-left faith in violent action.[34]

Violence against the junta came to be seen by some dissenting students as unavoidable and justifiable. For them, the campus itself became the battlefield. Throughout the November events, ultra-militant factions adopted violent tactics which they hoped would awaken the majority to the barbarism and brutality of the regime.[35] Other factions saw such clashes as a tool to preserve and encourage political dissent. One group (Movement of 20 October or *Kinima, 20is Oktomvri*)[36] argued that armed violence was the only effective weapon students and workers had in their hands with which to respond to state repression.[37] The movement reached its zenith when almost overnight it mobilized thousands of previously non-political workers and students. For three days and nights a worker-student alliance maintained permanent occupation of the Polytechnic building. Their uncompromising political language and heroic forms of action showed how vulnerable the regime could be to those who dared to challenge it. In the end, the November '73 revolt failed to spark off a larger conflagration because there was neither coherent strategy nor strong leadership to take organizational command of the movement.[38] The KKE communist party saw the protest through 'the prism of a narrow student event with limited capabilities and potentiality',[39] thus declining to emerge as the 'avant-guard detonator'. Seeking short-term political gains, KKE student leaders went instead to great lengths to prevent and stop all direct action.[40] That said, November 1973 was unmistakably a critical moment at which the course of Greek political and social history began to change in a concentrated and intense way, as the Athens Polytechnic events assumed symbolic significance, becoming 'the sole vehicle of collective expression and solidarity and public revulsion against oppression, injustice and limited freedom'.[41]

The radicalism of November ushered in a period of radical communist utopianism and acute political debate on conceptions of class, social structure and revolutionary strategy. The post-1973 impetus gave the far left an opportunity to present a fresh, radical and autonomous form of activism. More specifically, the radicalization of November 1973 and the general mood for fundamental change that followed the collapse of the Colonels' regime the following year reinforced their confidence and intensified their revolutionary utopianism.

Junta by another name? The 1974 Metapolitefsi *and the Revolutionary Left*

Metapolitefsi, as Greeks call the 1974 transition to multi-party democracy and political modernization, proved to be complex and difficult. Although Konstantinos Karamanlis commanded the popular assent of the country (54.4 per cent of the vote), he chose to adapt his ideas to the circumstances rather than the circumstances to his ideas. The presence of ministers associated with the fascist period in the Karamanlis cabinet showed the premier's political elasticity. Such strategy provoked strong resentment from the Athens press and intelligentsia.[42] At the same time, rumours and counter-rumours of aborted coups and assassination plots against Karamanlis abounded. Neo-fascist groups began a terrorist campaign with a series of bomb explosions and other attacks designed to create a climate of tension and instability. Cinema bombings became something of a neo-fascist hallmark. The years 1976 and 1978 were particularly critical. Faced with such challenges and uncertain of how far to go with the purge, the new regime did away with some regional state agencies,[43] but the *modus operandi* of the main apparatus remained unchanged. Not surprisingly, the governmental attempts to placate both the army and the public led to half-measures with regard to reform legislation and *apohountopoiisi* (dejuntification). The first years of *metapolitefsi* were thus marked by a curious amalgam of continuity and change. The symbols, the rhetoric and even the constitution changed, but without any systematic purge of the bureaucracy and the police apparatus; key sections of the state continued in the hands of the old order. When the Karamanlis government proved itself unable to deliver the promise of 'irreversible change', the credibility of the new republic was seriously weakened in the eyes of many ordinary Greeks, especially the students whose resistance to the military dictatorship had been instrumental in its destabilization. For those students on the extra-parliamentary left who had believed that *metapolitefsi* would bring about a broader democratic change, the sense of disappointment was even greater. Their disillusionment was to become a major source of instability and active discontent for the years to come. This was expressed in the form of protest movements, anti-establishment journalism and ultimately political violence.

From 1974 to 1976, a considerable number of revolutionary leftist groups emerged on the Greek post-junta political scene. These groups used violent rhetoric to justify the legitimacy of the revolutionary cause over the regime's perceived illegality and to denounce its gradualism and lack of structured political solutions.[44] Deeply hostile to the first post-junta Karamanlis government, they advocated wholesale political reform and the necessity of a viable democratic culture. Reflecting the various ideological divides within the revolutionary movement, these small-sized but very agitated groups were anarchist, Maoist[45] and Trotskyist.[46] Their common characteristic was an aggressive set of political attitudes and their principal enemy the regime itself. In spite of their size they tried in a number of ways to drive a fundamental re-analysis of the nature of society and class relations in post-dictatorial Greece. The far left, in other words, entered the 1974 *metapolitefsi* with guilt for not having done enough in the recent past and the conviction that with bolder tactics and a more aggressive political line, the time for revolutionary change was ripe. They proclaimed that the preceding years of organizational lethargy, bitter defeat and political isolation were about to herald a new phase of exciting political developments. Overall, between 1974 and late-1979, Trotskyist, Maoist and other extra-parliamentary extreme leftist groups constantly sought to transmit their specific messages, ideas and perspectives to 'the proletarian masses'. Despite their organizational defects and fragmented nature, all sections of the movement dreamed of a modern-day Bolshevik revolution. When it became clear that the political ground was infertile, some fanatical Marxist militants broke away from the movement and, behind organisational acronyms such as ELA, Group June '78, LEA and RO-17N, sought to impose 'deep and wholesale revolutionary change' through small-group urban terrorism.[47]

The Terrorists

Out of the ninety-five named left-wing terroristic signatures which appeared in the first years of *metapolitefsi*, only two were to make a long-term impact: the Revolutionary Popular Struggle (ELA) and 17N. ELA, which was the first group to emerge, argued that meaningful revolutionary change needed strategic direction from an armed vanguard of professional revolutionaries, since 'the conflagration that would eventually lead to the overthrow of the capitalist regime will be a long, hard and violent armed struggle'.[48] As a result, it set out from the start to form an operational vanguard to educate the 'passive' masses and convert them to the cause. ELA viewed itself as part of the international revolutionary movement, and thus counted imperialism, capitalism and fascism with all their various forms as its enemies. The group carried out hundreds of non-lethal, low-level bombings aimed at symbolic material targets, ranging from US military and business facilities, such as IBM, American Express, to EC and United Nations offices and foreign embassies. The group also used propaganda and 'factory management' targets to increase tension between strikers and the employers 'since conditions in the workplace are specifically designed by the capitalist bosses to dehumanize and isolate the working-class population'.[49]

ELA tried to present its violence as a form of organization which responded to material restraints and needs for the formation of a united command structure for the revolutionary forces. Rejecting completely the possibility of building socialism from within the existing system, ELA argued that:

> there have been plenty of dramatic examples in the past which demonstrate the illusion of power-seizure through peaceful parliamentary transition: the Greek civil war, Allende's Chile, the fascist Greece of 1967 and November 1973—all prove that the only path to the establishment of a dictatorship of a proletariat is the path of popular and revolutionary violence.[50]

Like ELA, 17N (which took its name from the night of 16/17 November 1973 when riot police backed up with tanks were sent in to put an end to the Athens Polytechnic occupation, causing the death of at least 34 students and the injury of another 800) viewed *metapolitefsi* as nothing more than a democratic facade: a massive confidence trick on the Greek nation by a political class which sought to legitimate its authority through the deliberate cultivation of fantasies of stability, transparency and pluralism. Both groups feared for the depoliticization of Greek society, distrusted parliamentary democracy and institutional discourse, were dogmatically anti-American, anti-NATO anti-EC, and made tireless efforts to expose the 'political doublespeak' of the Greek establishment. Operationally, however, 17N bore little resemblance to ELA. 17N's conception of the political environment was one of protest, resistance and aggressive violence. Between 1975 and 2000 the group's modus operandi incorporated high-profile assassinations, knee-cappings, armed raids, bombings and rocket attacks.[51] 17N saw the application of violence as the most effective way to crystallize public disaffection against the regime and embed itself in mainstream consciousness. 17N, at the same time, raised issues that have dominated post-1974 national politics: national sovereignty, anti-Americanism, Anglo-Saxon capitalism, Mediterranean socialism, European integration and international economic interdependence. The majority of these issues critically divided both sides of the Greek political spectrum, while others defined the parameters of the intellectual debate inside both the mainstream and extra-parliamentary left. Their presence in 17N's thematic agenda was part of the group's effort to attract attention and participate in public political debate. 17N aspired to be the ideological shaper and consciousness-raiser of the Greek working class, which it believed to be voiceless and politically unselfconscious in the post-junta parliamentary process. Unable, at the same time, to grasp the complexities of post-1974 political life and unwilling to accept the return of Karamanlis to power, 17N despised *metapolitefsi*. Even after the election of Andreas Papandreou in 1981 as the country's first ever socialist premier, the group used an accusatory terminology of betrayal, compromise and corruption. Papandreou's 'betrayal' was a strong and sufficient justification for terrorism in 17N's eyes. It became, in fact, the ideological catalyst which confirmed the group's view that 'popular revolutionary violence' and not parliamentarism was the only road to socialism. 17N came to regard the socialism of the Panhellenic Socialist Movement (PA.SO.K.), and US imperialism, as the two major enemies of the revolutionary cause. A communiqué depicted the Papandreou-led government as a nothing more than a committee managing the affairs of the Greek oligarchy.

Constantly questioning the authenticity of the country's conversion to liberal democracy, 17N attacked the entire political class as a hypocritical and demagogic clique pursuing its own interests at the expense of both the people and the nation. 17N leaders believed that the group was destined to become a symbol of defiance and play a historic role, but it never really managed to affect Greek political and social structures. In their obsessive attempts to articulate their goals and strategy, 17N ignored the fact that there was little enthusiasm among the people for the organization's theoretical models of revolution and root-and-branch critique of Greek parliamentary democracy. 17N's refusal to acknowledge this and its belief that ordinary people would eventually be converted to the revolution through an escalation of violence alienated almost every level of Greek society. The failure to ignite serious activity deepened the group's avant-gardism and led 17N to proceed in an elitist fashion. With no clear avenue of progress visible, and receiving media coverage on an extraordinary scale, the group gradually drifted into self-admiring exhibitionism, theatricalities and purposeless violence.

Both 17N and ELA used violence 'to effect a change in the body politic'. Entrenched by visions of class war and violent upheaval of the status quo, both 17N and ELA drew their belief that socialism in Greece could only be achieved through an armed struggle under the leadership of a revolutionary vanguard. Drawing on the complex traditions of Greek communism and the civil war legacy, the groups bitterly attacked the political structures of post-1974 Greek society. Their failure to attract support was largely because their politico-military rationale had little connection with contemporary political and social realities.

The end of ELA and 17N, when it finally came, did not diminish the attractiveness of prolonged terrorist violence as a tactical, strategic and psychopolitical tool. Although from an ideological standpoint both the ELA and 17N campaigns were a dramatic failure, revolutionary political behaviour remains, as will be seen in the following chapters on the country's post-17N generation of urban guerrilla groups, deeply embedded in the Greek armed struggle movement. Nostalgia and admiration for the revolutionary politics and gravitas of the older generation meant that the new groups, diverse in structure and character, quickly displayed their ability to reproduce essential ideological characteristics of the post-1974 adversarial militant tradition on the Greek political scene, continually seeking to raise tension and foment an atmosphere of near-insurrection.

3

GUERRILLA LEADER

DIMITRIS KOUFODINAS AND THE REVOLUTIONARY ORGANIZATION 17 NOVEMBER (17N)

The history of 17N terrorism[1] ended on 5 September 2002 when the group's leader of operations, Dimitris Koufodinas, turned himself in to the police after two months on the run following an explosion that led to the capture of 17N member Savvas Xiros and the breakup of the group. Koufodinas declared through a statement read out by his lawyer that he gave himself up:

> willingly to undertake the political responsibility of all 17N actions. I deny my guilt in the actions attributed to me the way they are in the indictment. The value that determined my personal course was my faith in the construction of revolutionary movement and my vision for a socialist society. I express my solidarity with all those who are in detention, justly or unjustly with regard to this case. For every fighter, dignity is a basic value and a title of honour.[2]

Koufodinas was born in 1958 in the village of Terpni, 45 kilometres from the city of Serres in northern Greece. Terpni was, as it remains today, a typical northern Greek village that prided itself on the ordinariness of its daily life and the unexciting decency of its people. In 1971, when Koufodinas was thirteen, his father moved the family to Athens at a time when the Greek capital was in turmoil because of the Colonels' dictatorial regime. The *Metapolitefsi*, the 1974 transition from dictatorship to democracy, seems to have had a strong impact on Koufodinas's early political formation. The 1974 transition, it must be emphasized, was not the result of a clear and sharp break with the Colonels' junta but the product of a whole range of compromises and negotiations between elite-level political actors and the military. The *Metapolitefsi*, or the 'junta by another name' as 17N called the transition in several communiqués, had a formative influence on Koufodinas's politicization, and his early involvement in student politics attests to that. A member of PA.SO.K.'s Socialist PAMK youth movement from secondary school, Koufodinas intensified his activism when he enrolled in 1977 at Athens University to read economics. Koufodinas is remembered by a secondary school friend, Nikos Giannopoulos, who testified in court, as 'someone whose depth and intellect were impressive for his age and who could have, had he stayed on course, landed himself at a later stage an important job in party-politics or the state bureaucracy'.[3] Another friend from his days of student activism remembered Koufodinas as a 'calm, articulate young man with guts and ideological consistency'.[4] Relatives also described Koufodinas as 'somebody who never liked upsetting people'.[5] Koufodinas broke family ties in 1983, almost a year before the attempted assassination of US Army Sergeant Robert Judd which, according to the indictment, was Koufodinas's operational debut with the group.[6]

The Trial

'I am not interested in this court's verdict. It is the people's verdict that will count in the end.'[7]

In the preface to his book *Inside Terrorism*, Bruce Hoffman admits that after studying terrorists and terrorism for more than two decades he is 'still struck by how disturbingly "normal" most terrorists seem' when you meet them. And when you actually sit down, Hoffman writes, and talk to these militants and persuade them to discuss their violent actions, many are not 'the wild-eyed fanatics or crazed killers' you would expect but 'highly articulate and extremely thoughtful individuals for whom terrorism is [or was] an entirely rational choice, often reluctantly embraced and then only after a considerable reflection and debate'.[8] Confirming Hoffman's argument, Koufodinas does not conform to the stereotype of the terrorist as a wild and irrational fanatic.[9] Never in the nine months of court proceedings did Koufodinas raise his voice above the pitch of natural conversation, and his every gesture and every word were controlled and measured. Although the presiding judge systematically asked him for answers to questions which would 'provide this court and Greek society as a whole with a clearer picture',[10] Koufodinas stubbornly resisted the temptation to say anything substantial (and possibly incriminating) about his comrades or the inner workings of the organization.[11] In his court testimony Koufodinas declared:

> I won't do what you would want me to do. I won't even bother entering your logic. Our morality doesn't accept logics of cooperation and squealing. I will say nothing about my role in connection to the organization. I won't even begin to tell you in which operations I had or I had no role. And I will say nothing about any of my co-defendants. This is my stand and will hold on to it until the end, irrespective of any personal cost.[12]

Described by several 17N members in their testimony in the summer of 2002 as the key link between the group's historic leadership and the operatives, Koufodinas acknowledged before the court responsibility for all of 17N's grim legacy, but he refused at any stage of the proceedings to recognize that his group had been completely wrong in its analysis of Greek society. On the contrary, Koufodinas declared that he remained confident of ultimate victory even though he accepted that as far as the organization's operations were concerned 17N was finished. Koufodinas argued that 'from a historical perspective, and given the revolutionary movement's course in this country, the end of 17N's story [had] yet to be written'.[13]

Koufodinas believed that 17N and 17N alone continued to represent in Greece a pure and undefiled Marxist-Leninist faith, dismissing the universal designation of them as terrorists and of their actions as terrorism. Challenging the court's tendency in depicting their acts as acts of senseless barbarity devoid of any serious political content, Koufodinas argued that 'this present court does not wish to and cannot put 17N on trial for what 17N really was'.[14] In his view, 17N 'was, as the group had persistently stated from the very beginning, an organization of simple, popular fighters. And since it came from the guts of the populace, it was the populace's voice that 17N listened to, and it was the populace's own interests that it tried to serve.'[15]

The Early Years

Going back to the group's armed debut in 1975 and the assassination of the CIA's station chief in Athens, Richard Welch, Koufodinas tried to explain where 17N drew inspiration and motivation from for its campaign.[16] 'In December '75,' he stated, 'a group of fighters decided to execute the CIA's station chief in Athens.' In the words of Koufodinas there:

> couldn't be a more clear and justified action. The CIA's station chief was and remains the long hand of American power in our country. Running a fifth column of a few hundred agents positioned in neuralgic posts inside the government, the state bureaucracy, the army, the political parties and the media, he controls and directs the political, social and economic life of our country in relation to the interests of the USA. The Greek people know full well what the CIA was all about, know the role it has played since the civil war. [The role it had played] in every election, especially the 1961 election of rigging and violence; in the assassination of [Greek MP] Lambrakis, and the military junta and the tragedy of Cyprus. Why has the Cyprus dossier not been opened yet? Whatever happened to your justice and your democracy? Why so much selectivity for what is a crime and who is really a criminal? Who let the [junta] torturers walk free? Was it the people or was it your independent justice? For, the Greek people know exactly why the CIA's station chief in Greece was executed. What they didn't know exactly was who was were behind this action and that was thanks to a campaign of disinformation, distortion and disorientation by the government, the political parties and the media. When the campaign of 17N began, a campaign of disinformation began with it and still continues to this day.[17]

Throughout, Koufodinas tried to conceal the fact that 17N possessed as a group little capacity or inclination for organizing mass action. The group, he conceded with overdue proletarian modesty, 'never considered itself to be the centre of revolution, nor did it consider that its modes of action were the only appropriate ones,'[18] confirming the view that even if a revolutionary situation had arrived in Greece, the group would have lacked the organizational strength to exploit it since it was neither a guerrilla force nor an effective popular political movement. Koufodinas, however, described 17N as an organization of:

> the revolutionary left, a part of the left which believes that the present-day social system cannot ease the social inequalities simply because it provokes and accentuates them. A system that cannot solve the problem of unemployment simply because it creates unemployment and needs to do so. A

system that cannot efface war and conflict simply because it feeds on both. A system that cannot support the equal development of all nations simply because it relies on the unequal treatment and exploitation of the backward, underdeveloped countries. A system that doesn't care about the ecological damage that it causes on our planet. And a system that shows no respect to different cultures and different races simply because it obeys the God of money and profit.[19]

Such a system, Koufodinas asserted, 'couldn't be reformed, couldn't be democratized nor could be humanized: it had to be overthrown through a socialist revolution'.[20] At the same time, however, he recognized that finding a political route to it had been 'for the past two centuries the central issue within the left and the main area of contention between the reformist and revolutionary left'.[21]

'Fighting for the Poor, the Weak and the Exploited'

Commitment to ideology as a guide for political action pervaded Koufodinas's court testimony. Advocating revolutionary violence as an ideological response to declining radicalism and reformism, Koufodinas deplored 'all those who had turned their back on revolutionary activism out of sheer opportunism and bourgeois convenience'.[22] In Koufodinas's analysis, 'the difference between those who had chosen the path to revolution and those who hadn't was neither a theoretical nor an abstract one', since choosing the path of revolution meant 'choosing to fight for the poor, the weak and the exploited'.[23] At the same time, in an attempt to impose retrospective historical significance on what 17N was and did, Koufodinas claimed that 'the Left which 17N belonged to was the left of Lenin, Che Guevara and Velouchiotis; the left of the October, Spanish, Chinese and Cuban revolutions; the left of the anticolonial revolutions in Algeria and Vietnam, the left of May '68 and November '73. The left of urban guerrilla warfare.'[24]

One of Koufodinas's most insistent themes during the nine months of the trial was 17N's 'struggle' against 'American military imperialism'. In combative tone, Koufodinas presented the attacks of the group against US targets as a challenging response to American bullying and barbarity on Greek soil and in the region as a whole. American imperialism, he added, had brought nothing but chaos and butchery not only in Greece but in most parts of the planet, and the only way left to the people of the world to resist was 'asymmetric guerrilla warfare'. For 17N's operational chief, asymmetric guerrilla warfare was premised on the prototype guerrilla assumption that a sustained rate of small-scale military operations could generate a degree of coercive psychological pressure disproportionate to their destructive consequences. Koufodinas was convinced that asymmetric guerrilla warfare would sooner rather than later result in the creation of 'many Vietnams and that could prove the Achilles' heel of this arrogant hyper-armed empire'.[25] In this context, Koufodinas also said that for the past twenty-seven years, 17N had made it its central task 'to discredit and humiliate the mythologized [US] secret services, quash and crush their image as the formidable Hollywood super agents, something which explains their hysterical rage and vindictiveness against us'.[26] The condescending language Koufodinas used to describe the US intelligence services was reminiscent of 17N's provocative 'Come and get us, if you really can' communiqué in 1999, released a week after reports in the Greek media that US intelligence had provided the Simitis government with a list of 17N members.[27]

For Koufodinas, present-day Greece was not very far ideologically from the post-civil war Greece of the 1960s. One did not have to be a historian of modern Greece, he said, in order to recognize that the deep polarizations running from top to bottom of Greece's inequality-riven society were the product of 'a state that used scandalous taxation and banking systems to direct the capital made by many to the pockets of the few, driving the country into economic decline, stagnation and today's inevitable deindustrialization'.[28] There was no shadow of doubt in Koufodinas's mind that Greece was run by thieves and that the people mainly responsible for turning the Greek polity into a kleptocracy were the country's established political elites. Having declared that Greek politicians on all sides had cheating in their bloodstream, Koufodinas also made plain that he particularly deplored the fact that the parties of the left had long been 'assimilated by the present political regime, and had in fact become the regime's left-side crutches, selling out struggles and letting achievements of past decades go to waste'.[29]

From Karl Marx to Aris Velouchiotis

The resort to violence was for Koufodinas a reasonable and calculated response to a resigned, defeatist and inept left which reneged on its own principles. 'But beyond this left', Koufodinas argued, 'there also exists the anti-regime left, the left which refuses turning the other cheek too; the left which believes that the solution to the deep flaws of the system and the political, social and cultural crisis can only be a revolutionary solution'.[30] Taking his theme further, Koufodinas paraphrased from Karl Marx's *Das Kapital* and *The Communist Manifesto* in order to rationalize 17N's campaign of violence and argue that according to Marx, violence of that kind was not terrorism.[31]

The strategies of guerrilla groups of Latin America, the Tupamaros in particular, were also employed by 17N's operational leader to explain how the group came to see the use and practice of organized military force as an effective instrument of policy. Koufodinas seemed to agree with the strategic approach that for groups like 17N, a sophisticated understanding of the utility of the military instrument and how it can best be exploited in a psychological sense was of catalytic importance if the groups' political goals were ever to be fulfilled. When 17N commandos, Koufodinas said:

> raided the Vyronas police station and the National War Museum making off with anti-tank weapons and bazookas, and the same when they entered the Sykourio military warehouse stealing 60 rockets, grenades, bullets and other explosives and all this without firing a single bullet, they demonstrated that 17N was not only a self-appointed group but also a group that had the appropriate resources at its disposal to engage in revolutionary armed struggle.[32]

For Koufodinas, one could say anything one liked about 17N, except that it was something other than what it always claimed to be and showed itself to be in all of its actions. 17N's activity, he further argued, 'had the very same characteristics with the activity of the [Greek] resistance'. Koufodinas did not attempt to present himself as a modern-day Aris Velouchiotis, the charismatic guerrilla leader and founder of ELAS (the Greek People's Liberation Army), but it quickly became apparent that he idolized Velouchiotis. 'When Aris would enter a village and give under the nose of the Germans a speech in the village square with his armed partisans in formation, he was both demonstrating that armed resistance was possible and cultivating the ground for further activity.'[33] By connecting ELAS's military aims and practices to those of 17N, Koufodinas wanted to show that the group's armed struggle taking place 'in a country which has experienced humiliation, exclusion, state-terrorism, the absolute power of plutocrats, policemen and military judges' was merely defensive. 17N attacked targets, Koufodinas said:

> which symbolised imperialism and capitalism. And, yes, we did manage to terrorize them if you consider that Washington spent more on protection for its Athens embassy than it did anywhere else in the world. [And if you consider] that the security services of big countries in the West kept on sending their best experts and kept on offering astronomical sums of money for information that would lead to an arrest. That the Greek big industrialists and tycoons would build fortresses and have armies of bodyguards. All these people—and we're talking about a few thousands of them—were really terrorized by us and for that we are very proud.[34]

Koufodinas also denied charges that 17N had held the country to ransom by terror. 17N violence was, as he put it, very carefully controlled and discriminate and 'the majority of the Greek people did not go to sleep every night fearing that their lives were in danger from 17N'. For Koufodinas, it was rather the regime's violence that 'provoked fear and terror to the entire population and it was the violence of the state security mechanisms which caused loneliness and human degradation'.[35] 17N's operations chief also charged that 'the regime used the term "terrorism" to cover up the reality of its own violence and try at the same time to defame the [group's] popular anti-violence.'[36]

Koufodinas took this theme further by dealing with the question of how far the military instrument could be manipulated to achieve the group's political goals. Declaring that 17N had 'rightly been characterized by many as an organization of moderation', he went on to explain that the group was never under any illusions about 'the movement's level of development and that was precisely why it did not declare total war on all fronts'.[37] Although he failed to acknowledge directly the fact that the military means at the group's disposal were always limited, Koufodinas observed that 17N 'never made full use of all available resources because the group did not want to rush things and also because it never confused its goals with reality and violence with present political circumstances'.[38] According to Koufodinas, it was 'within this logic that 17N made no attempts to attack at the heart of the Greek state so there could be no exaggerated polarization'[39] which would have (even though Koufodinas refused to admit this) precipitated the group's undoing, as had happened in Italy with the Red Brigades.[40]

Propaganda and 'Political Results'

The 17N leadership was influenced by the Red Brigades' view that military actions 'are intended as armed propaganda' and that violence was used to both 'illustrate new possibilities of political action and secure some form of political recognition'.[41] To Koufodinas it was clear that every single armed action was an effective instrument of propaganda aimed at building momentum and gaining support. 17N's operations chief further argued that the propaganda value of a military action was determined by the type and nature of that action. Armed action, he said, could only carry the group and the movement forward to its objectives if the choice of target was one that 'spoke for itself and also one that ordinary people immediately understood and identified with'.[42] Mapping out certain parameters of 17N's strategic formulation, Koufodinas insisted that the target selection must also be of a sort that 'exposes and deligitimates the regime without having any negative political or material consequences for the workers and the mass movement'.[43] Koufodinas saw 17N military activity as:

> inextricably linked to the wide popular masses and their everyday problems and therefore strikes were directed against targets like the tax system of the swindler state or against the regime of public hospital doctors whose lack of ethos and humanity forced patients into big doctors and private clinics spending huge sums ... 17N's activity also had a symbolic value. It selected targets-symbols of power and authority in every political, economic and social sphere: representatives of institutional mechanisms and of imperialistic hegemony and capitalist exploitation, corrupted politicians and civil servants, thieves of social wealth and public property.[44]

Koufodinas was equally emphatic about the 'political results' that came from 17N's activity. In his words, 17N's actions were generally seen as 'just social defence against' agents of anti-national interest such as the plutocratic oligarchy whose 'deeds were causing serious social damage'.[45] Koufodinas asked the judges somewhat sarcastically 'whether society or individual members of that society should have the right to defend themselves against such acts of heavy social cost, especially when your own institutional mechanisms have been doing nothing about it'.[46] As far as Koufodinas was concerned, 17N 'functioned as a counterbalance against such an all-powerful regime while articulating at the same time the message that some people still resist and will always continue to resist'.[47]

For him, 17N actions against the powerful mechanisms of the regime had a rejuvenating effect on the Greek populace's sense of dignity and pride'.[48] Koufodinas's point was to show that 17N actions were 'judged by the Greek people on the basis of their past humiliating, oppressive and exploitative experiences, as actions of self-defence and popular justice. And this is why 17N's actions were met with social and popular acceptance.'[49]

Preoccupied by the idea and reality of 'guerrilla warfare as the only revolutionary method of intervention available to what are on the whole weak revolutionary forces',[50] Koufodinas believed his group to have been the ideological shaper and consciousness-raiser of the Greek working class which he thought to be voiceless and politically unselfconscious. Koufodinas saw the application of violence as the most effective way to crystallize public disaffection against 'an undemocratic society which lacks compassion and doesn't care about its weak and ailing members'.[51] Pointing to the fact that 20 per cent of Greek people were living below the poverty line and another 15 per cent were unemployed, Koufodinas said that he continued to believe in the absolute validity of the armed struggle. 'Can violent actions take place in a democracy?' he asked. 'Would someone want to overthrow such democracy? Of course, he would, since it is a self-negating system of democracy... a democracy that refutes itself...'.[52]

Identity and Morality

Koufodinas repeatedly rejected the media's charges of the group being psychotic ideologues fighting a hopeless war. To Koufodinas it was clear that 'an armed revolutionary' was not a 'maniac of violence, a lunatic, a lover of guns and killings'. Treating the court to a philosophical *tour d'horizon*, 17N's operations chief argued that a revolutionary 'chooses violence as a direct response through political analyses'.[53] 'And once he has chosen to go down that path,' Koufodinas added, 'he has the obligation, if he is true to himself and to his ideas, to go all the way.'[54] Koufodinas presented the armed revolutionary as someone 'whose life choices are actually made against his personal interests'.[55] As someone 'who, having to overcome his strong instincts for self-survival, he seeks a closer encounter with a biologically unreasonable existence—unreasonable simply because he is in danger of losing his freedom.'[56] Rather than advancing the view that a revolutionary's existence begins to have meaning only once he joins a group in which he belongs and has faith, Koufodinas argued somewhat paradoxically that 'this actually happens at the point when the fighter is forced to experience a deep and unbearable contradiction between love for life and the necessity for action against it.'[57] Koufodinas, at the same time, did not want to be seen retreating behind the defence that the fighter had to 'pay a very high price of pain for this contradiction', as he phrased it. The price was undoubtedly high, he added, but this was compensated by the fact that the fighter was 'taking part in a struggle against protogenic violence—violence that denies man his inner essence, dehumanizes him and ultimately sinks him into barbarity'.[58]

Prison

Unlike the group's chief ideologue, Alexandros Giotopoulos, who denied participation in 17N, Koufodinas took responsibility for the entire 17N experience and defended its actions from inside prison. 'I could have escaped, if I wanted to,' he said in a newspaper interview:

> and gone on to build a new life away from all the things that might have betrayed me. But that would have gone against revolutionary morality, my own ideas and beliefs. I couldn't leave my comrades, one of them badly injured [Savvas Xiros], with whom we fought together and shared dreams, hopes and disappointments to become hostages at the hands of a revengeful state while I was to be enjoying a dishonourable freedom. I could not let people who had nothing to do with the organization or came to contact with it without knowing to be wrongly accused. I could not abandon my partner [Aggeliki Sotiropoulou] and let her go through what she was going through because of my own choices. Nor could I let her be used as a pressure tool against me. Rather than opting for the security of silence and exile, I chose to show up, take political responsibility of my choices and defend them at all costs.[59]

Koufodinas was forty-four when he was taken to Korydallos maximum security prison, where he has continued, unlike the rest of the imprisoned 17N members whose 'revolutionary spirit' quickly evaporated, to assert his political status with the help of his defence lawyer[60] through carefully selected interviews with the Greek media, and to resist state criminalization through sporadic hunger strikes and protests against prison rules and procedures.

Like the German Red Army Faction (RAF) in Stuttgart-Stanheim prison and the French Action Directe (AD) in the Fleury-Merogis Maison d'Arrêt des Femmes, the 17N prisoners had their own high-security wing built next to the female wing of Korydallos prison. Koufodinas's partner, Aggeliki Sotiropoulou, who herself spent fifteen months in Korydallos before her release, described the 17N special wing as 'an underground corridor of 16 square meters with a metallic box for a yard and sky high walls and barbed-wire. A modern systematic torture chamber that aims to physically and mentally destroy them.'[61] In an interview with *Eleftherotypia*, the newspaper that 17N used to send its communiqués for publication, Koufodinas described Korydallos prison as a 'specialized solitary confinement'.[62] Speaking of the inherently dehumanizing nature of imprisonment, Koufodinas accepted that prison conditions 'were always going to be wretched, but it was "the prison inside the prison" that made it particularly vengeful'.[63] Special prison units such as the one housing the 17N militants, he added, aimed 'at hurting the personality and consciousness of the prisoners'. We will not stop, he added, 'condemning the special prisons as means of controlling ideas and we will keep on joining our voices to all the voices out there who fight against their legitimization and expansion.'[64] Koufodinas repeatedly endorsed the claim that there was 'a section of society out there that resists and fights. And as long there are people who resist, no special forms of barbarity can be easily imposed on society's consciousness.'[65]

In his newspaper interviews from prison, Koufodinas repeatedly returned to the revolutionary movement and to the activities of Greece's post-17N generation of militant groups such as Revolutionary Struggle (RS), which proved Koufodinas's rather pessimistic prognosis wrong when he had stated back in 2003 that 'perhaps, in ten to fifteen years' time, a new generation of fighters might relaunch the struggle'.[66] Surprisingly, RS picked up the baton of violence from 17N before the latter's trial had even come to an end, with a barrage of bomb attacks that shocked a Greek security apparatus under the impression that 17N's dismantling had brought the final victory over terrorism in the country.[67] Speaking in 2007, Koufodinas said that 17N's demise had left 'a gap of revolutionary praxis wide open which groups such as the Sect of Revolutionaries and Revolutionary Struggle were trying to fill, or some part of it at least. Whether they will succeed, and how, it is too early to say.'[68] Speaking of RS in particular, Koufodinas said that 'although he did not see himself as an analyst of models of revolutionary activity designed and implemented by others' the group had 'so far, shown it has political depth and a good selection of targets'.[69] Koufodinas, however, was explicit that the new groups were 'not a natural progression from 17N' because the historical realities and the political environment were considerably different, but he said that should not prevent the new organizations from studying the older groups to learn from them and avoid making the same mistakes.[70] 'Without wishing to come across as paternalistic', Koufodinas's advice to the new groups was to follow 17N's example and 'make use of history where they could'.[71]

Koufodinas, a student and life-long admirer of Latin American urban revolutionary movements in general and the Uruguayan Tupamaros in particular, taught himself Spanish inside his Korydallos prison cell in order to translate *Memorias del Calabozo*, the prison diaries of two Tupamaros guerrilla leaders, Mauricio Rosencof and Niato Fernández Huidobro.[72] The Tupamaros (MLN-T),[73] 'a large urban guerrilla revolutionary movement which combined political violence with virtue,' writes Koufodinas in the foreword to the Greek edition, 'was not an exotic creation of an elitist intelligentsia but rather a response to the violence of the oligarchy against the people. It was, if not the popular movement's creation, a solid part of the movement.'[74] Koufodinas lauded the MLN-T's technical efficiency, 'economic use of violence' and use of the modern city as a theatre of revolutionary warfare.[75] As he further explained, MLN-T, primarily interested in the symbolic impact of its attacks, 'always tried to combine the act with a specific message that the act was meant to convey', calculating at the same time how the message would be received by its target group and the wider public.[76]

Myth and Revolution

'Why did you kill my husband?' Dora Bakoyiannis, mayor of Athens at the time and widow of an 17N victim, Pavlos Bakoyiannis, assassinated in 1989, asked Koufodinas. 'Read our proclamation,' came the laconic reply from him. 'It sets out the reasons very well.'[77] This type of remark was typical of 17N thinking and underlined the fact that the group's conception of the political arena was not one where men and women are invited to choose freely between competing ideas and visions through argument and debate, but one characterized by a series of unmovable truths to which people should owe allegiance. It was Koufodinas's philosophy of the gun that for almost three decades underpinned 17N's campaign of terrorism. Ignoring the principle that violence 'should not take the place of the political purpose, nor obliterate it',[78] 17N continued the sporadic killing and wounding of high-profile targets as the most effective means available to crystallize public disaffection against the regime and embed itself in mainstream consciousness.

An emblematic personality of 17N terrorism, Koufodinas embraced the view that Greece's 'self-negating democracy' necessitated exactly the kind of political violence they had undertaken. Obsessively clinging to his conviction that 17N took on 'the capitalist state and its agents', Koufodinas maintained that it was attempting to create an insurrectionary mood which would empower Greek people into revolutionary political action.

Constantly questioning the authenticity of Greece's 1974 conversion to liberal democracy, Koufodinas attacked the entire political class as a hypocritical and demagogic clique pursuing its own interests at the expense of both the people and the nation. According to Koufodinas, 17N's violence was nothing less than an audacious protest which discredited and humiliated the Greek establishment and the US government. Unapologetic about the group's murderous record, Koufodinas told the court that death was fundamentally not a moral problem but a political one and therefore 'labels such as assassins and deplorable killers that people place upon us, cannot really define our actions'.[79]

Koufodinas's apologia confirmed that 17N had seen the political environment as one of callous, mindless violence. Repeating mechanically the same narrow verbal formula of violent anticapitalist revolutionary warfare, Koufodinas conveniently ignored the fact that there had been on the part of 17N no grand strategy, no master plan, no focused campaign, no attack on the heart of the state. In fact, what 17N had been waging for the past twenty-seven years was not a war of psychological attrition but a sporadic assassination campaign. One other thing that Koufodinas's apologia confirmed was that he lived in a closed, self-referential world where terrorism had become a way of life. An armed revolutionary, he declared, is someone who 'takes up arms because he cherishes life and not the contrary', leaving unanswered the question of how a fringe group with no community support, which had brought nothing but butchery and suffering, could 'defend life from those who abuse and humiliate it', as he characteristically put it.[80]

Koufodinas's stubborn refusal throughout and after the trial to confront reality made him speak like a man whose entire sense of life revolved around the belief that destiny had somehow granted him this extraordinary privilege that he must guard well and pass on at some historical point. Feeling himself to be a genuine instrument of history, Koufodinas advanced the view that it did not matter that there could never be a military victory as long as 17N 'intervened' and 'resisted'. In that sense, 17N had been impervious to political logic since it did not matter to the group that its campaign of terrorist violence was anachronistic, incoherent and doomed to failure from its very inception. And it did not matter that murdering people in a fantasy war with the Greek establishment was wrong and pointless. For Koufodinas and the majority of his 17N comrades what was and remained important was the act of resistance itself. And the notion that blood and death, even one's own, would somehow carry the mission forward.

4

EXIT 17N

PATROKLOS TSELENTIS AND SOTIRIS KONDYLIS

Despite the adage 'once a terrorist always a terrorist', terrorists can and frequently do give up committing acts of violence. This is a crucially important observation that offers much potential insight to policymakers and counterterrorism specialists battling with the current generation of terrorists, who should consider what lessons we can learn from terrorists who desist. Under what circumstances do terrorists choose to terminate their connection with terrorism? There has been a great deal of scholarship on why individuals or groups resort to terrorism.[1] Yet, there has been comparatively little analysis on why individual terrorists end their involvement in violent activities.[2] Given the potential value of such analysis for counterterrorism efforts, understanding individual exit from a terrorist organization should be viewed as having the same urgency as understanding the reasons why people join such organizations and why they choose to remain in them.[3] Addressing the question of why individual members of a terrorist organization give up their violence has become increasingly important as the jihadist threat evolves into a less hierarchical and more diffuse cellular system.[4] As such, the psychology of the terrorist, the issues of group identity, loyalty and the vulnerabilities of individual members to outside influences are relevant to choices about legislative initiatives and counterterrorism strategies.

The 17N terrorist group provides an untouched pool of data from which to draw preliminary conclusions to the above question. This chapter analyses the life histories of Patroklos Tselentis and Sotiris Kondylis, former 17N members in order to look for causes of disengagement, dissociation and repentance and search for lessons that would be useful against the current generation of terrorists and terrorist organizations.

Patroklos Tselentis

Patroklos Tselentis was arrested on 25 July 2002. His arrest came three weeks after the bomb carried by Savvas Xiros exploded prematurely in Athens's port of Piraeus. Tselentis, forty-two at the time, although one of the last 17N suspected members to be caught, was the first to be taken directly to the appellate courts to be charged and cross-examined.[5] Appearing before special magistrate Leonidas Zervobeakos, Tselentis asked and received three days extension to prepare his testimony which subsequently became central to the state's case against the organization's two main leaders: Alexandros Giotopoulos, 17N's chief ideologue and Dimitris Koufodinas, the group's head of operations. Tselentis had become 17N's biggest *pentito*.

Based primarily on Italian anti-terrorism legislation utilized during the Italy's 'Years of Lead', Greek anti-terrorism legislation encouraged voluntary collaboration and cooperation with the authorities and the renunciation of terrorist aims and methods. In Italy, the basic model of *pentimento* was established in December 1979 when, at the end of the worst year for political violence in a decade, the Italian government introduced the penitence law which offered a substantial reduction in sentence to anyone charged with crimes of terrorism or subversion who turned state's evidence. Obtaining the reduction required a full confession, unequivocal rupture of all contact with terrorist organizations and active collaboration in identifying former accomplices and averting further violence. If a confession enabled police and magistrates to gather 'decisive proof' to incriminate conspirators, its author was entitled to a reduction between one-third and one-half of the normal prison term: the penalty for murder could be reduced from life imprisonment to a sentence between twelve and twenty years.[6]

Most people, and terrorists are generally no exception, do not ordinarily engage in reprehensible conduct unless they justify to themselves the morality of their actions. Tselentis constituted no exception. He joined 17N in 1983 and lasted until the autumn of 1988, having participated in eleven operations, the last being the 17N raid of an Athens police station in August 1988. According to the 17N pentito, by the end of 1987 he had reached a crossroads and could no longer justify the group's activities nor his direct role and participation in those activities.

In his seminal *Why Men Rebel*, Ted Robert Gurr argued some time ago that most participants in political violence, revolutionary or otherwise, 'do not carry complex ideologies around in their heads.'[7] Tselentis belonged to a long list of European terrorists from a working-class background who became involved in left-wing political activism during their university years. Tselentis's family background like Renato Curcio's and Margherita Cagol's of the Italian BR, was inauspicious. Like his Italian counterparts, he came from a stable, quiet, conservative and close-kit family. Born in the island of Kefallonia, a typical Greek holiday destination, the Tselentis family relocated to Athens to the working-class area of Korydallos, when Tselentis's older brother gained a place at the university. Ironically, Korydallos is also the home of the Greek capital's largest maximum-security prison, where Tselentis and the other 17N members would later be kept. After graduating from high school, Tselentis enrolled in Athens University at a time of student unrest and agitation over long-standing and unresolved issues regarding the democratization of the educational system, improved educational facilities and the abolition of legislation which restricted academic freedom. Student radicalization would often culminate in demonstrations, general assemblies and rallies throughout the city and in faculty occupations, some of which went on for months, bringing the entire university machine to a halt. By the end of 1980, the discord had intensified with the students' anger spreading beyond academic concerns. In November 1980, during a march to the American embassy to mark the anniversary of the November 1973 Polytechnic student revolt, running street battles broke out between demonstrators and the police, who responded with stun grenades and volleys of tear gas that left clouds of the chemicals hovering over central Syntagma Square. In the heavy clashes and street fighting that went on for hours, two people died and hundreds of demonstrators were injured. The violent and over-confrontational conduct of the police towards the demonstrators further radicalized Tselentis's approach to politics. 'The events at the Polytechnic had a radicalizing effect on me. I was lucky not to have been hurt during the clashes, but many friends of mine, and many friends of theirs, sustained serious injuries at the hands of the police.'[8] At the same time, Tselentis began to lose confidence in the ability and willingness of the mainstream left parties to push for meaningful change. It had become 'obvious to the naked eye that the existing left had accepted the idea of playing by the bourgeois political rules, and were not interested in the fundamental change of the social status quo. I then became convinced that the remedy for the inequities and malfunctions of Greek society could only come through violence against the state apparatus.'[9]

Meeting Dimitris Koufodinas

Tselentis first met Koufodinas in 1982 during an Athens University general assembly. Koufodinas at the time was, according to Tselentis, heavily involved in university activism, coordinating delegations and organizing petitions, leafleting, protest marches and public meetings. Although most of the protests took classical forms of democratic public expression, the period remained disruptive, disorderly and often violent. Tselentis's recollections of this phase include very strong memories of excited discussions between student activists looking for a new organization and new forms of action by which to disrupt the system and promote collective action and mass mobilization:

> There were a lot of young people at that time who had become disillusioned with constitutional structures and the institutional left and were willing to engage in more radical forms of action. Some of us, in fact, were fascinated by the activity of illegal militant groups operating at the time and believed that we should help in whatever way we could.[10]

Tselentis and Koufodinas would discuss issues for hours, sometimes days, and attend marches and demonstrations together. As their friendship developed and became stronger, so did their discussions about the armed struggle. 'Koufodinas would show me', Tselentis recalled:

> printed material from semi-illegal organizations, which propagandized yet refrained from using violent activity and I remember being very excited about the whole thing. Having said that, in the demonstrations and street marches in which I took part—and they were many—I always made sure that I was never in the frontline where the clashes with the police would take place. I never physically clashed with the police and never threw a Molotov cocktail although I was happy and supportive of those who did.[11]

As time went on, the idea of political violence, aided by the close contact with and discussions between himself and Koufodinas, must have begun to work its way into Tselentis's mind. When Tselentis told Koufodinas that he had come to the conclusion that he was now prepared and willing 'to sacrifice [his] life and [his] future to fight for a cause and for fundamental social change', Koufodinas said in return that:

> he, himself, belonged to a group of like-minded individuals who were convinced that for Greek society to change radical political action was needed. A group that, unlike the existing parties and political groups, would not shy away from operating outside the law and engaging in protracted violent struggle in order to radicalize the masses and challenge the social order.[12]

Having convinced Tselentis of the necessity of turning to armed struggle Koufodinas then proceeded to gradually introduce the new recruit to selected members of that group, including Christodoulos Xiros, the older brother of Savvas and Yiannis Skandalis, who later died in a random car accident.

Tselentis's First Operation

The extent to which a terrorist identifies himself with the ideology of the group 'is commensurate with the sacrifices and risks he is prepared to make on its behalf, up to and including his life'.[13] Tselentis's decision to move into illegality and fight for the revolution was one compelled by a sense of destiny and adventure. Fascinated by the image of the armed struggle of a small band against the many, he wanted to risk for all others in a just cause. Like many before him, he had no grasp at the time of what the real life of an urban guerrilla might be like, but this very leaping into the dark must have also been a strong motive. The first action in which Tselentis took part was a bank robbery. Koufodians, a student and fervent admirer of Latin American revolutionaries, made sure that Carlos Marighella's manual on 'expropriation' was closely followed, though modified to local requirements and conditions.[14]

Despite several weeks of preparation, the operation on Christmas Eve 1984 against the National Bank of Greece branch in Kato Petralona did not go as planned. As Koufodinas, Xiros and Skandalis were about to exit the bank carrying bags of money, a police guard engaged with them. Koufodinas, who was dressed as police officer, drew a Berreta pistol and shot the guard dead before making it to the getaway car. Tselentis, who as a novice was taken along to provide cover, and most probably to be tested under pressure, witnessed the incident from the bank's entrance. Koufodinas decisiveness and ruthlessness under pressure not only fitted with BR member Patrizio Peci's description of a successful commando group, 'tense but not nervous, calm but not relaxed, decisive but not foolhardy', but also made Tselentis realize that he was part of something much bigger and more dangerous than he originally thought.[15] A meeting arranged by Koufodinas a few months after the National Bank of Greece incident, where Tselentis met for the first time Alexandros Giotopoulos, the group's ideologue, confirmed any remaining suspicions that that the group he had joined was 17N.

Tselentis found membership in 17N an exhilarating experience. His involvement with a group which 'exercised at the time a tremendous fascination on the left at large, on the media and the national imagination' made him 'proud'. 'I was in the front line, fighting for something I believed was worth fighting for'.[16] The group, Tselentis said, 'saw the "near revolution" of the 1973 Polytechnic uprising[17] as a defining historical moment and sought to recreate it'. According to Tselentis, the group's aim was 'to foster revolutionary consciousness and provide leadership and training to the revolutionary mass movement which in due course would take up the arms and challenge the existing order'.[18] At the same time, however, Tselentis, and most probably the rest of the group, was under no illusion that 17N were ever going to find themselves in a position of actually seizing power and governing. 17N's role, as Tselentis saw it at the time, was to 'persuade parts of the movement to consider taking up arms'.[19]

Tselentis explained that 17N's concept of urban guerrilla strategy was based on the recognition that without revolutionary initiatives there would be no revolutionary orientation for the popular movement when conditions for revolutionary struggle were more favourable. Having accepted that the political possibilities were not to be fully recognised until armed struggle was recognized as a political goal, 17N's primary aim was to create the connection between legality and illegality, offering the movement the necessary organizational structure. Violent disagreement with political rules was to become the basic mental frame around which 17N members sought to construct a viable revolutionary strategy. 17N's military actions, the Greek *pentito* explained, were:

> intended as armed propaganda, used to demonstrate to the populace and the movement, new possibilities of political action and armed interven-

tion. It was a way to persuade society that change could only be achieved through violent revolutionary action. As such, the selection of targets had to be easily understood and widely accepted by the populace.[20]

The Momferatos Assassination

Tselentis's first involvement in an assassination came in February 1985. Following closely the idea that the selection of target must speak for itself so that ordinary people would immediately understand and identify with it, the group targeted and killed, in the centre of Athens, Nikos Momferatos, publisher of the country's biggest selling conservative newspaper *Apogevmatini* together with his driver-bodyguard. 17N targeted Momferatos because, in his capacity as the President of the Association of Athens Newspaper Publishers, he was held responsible for the media's campaign of 'misinformation and systematic distortion of truth' against the Greek people.[21] Momferatos, who had served as a Minister of Industry during the military junta, was described by 17N as 'a fascist-junta man and a CIA agent' who instead of being imprisoned for his involvement in the dictatorship's crimes, brazenly used his power as a newspaper owner to manipulate Greek public opinion.[22]

Speaking about the operation and his role in the attack, Tselentis explained that once Koufodinas and Giotopoulos had picked the spot, a quiet and narrow street between his office and residence, where Momferatos and his driver would be ambushed, duties and responsibilities were allocated to each member of the commando unit and discussion would then follow on handwritten drafts of the communiqué stating the reasons behind the attack. 'The hand-written draft was read out several times, we would talk about it, make observations, change bits before Koufodinas took it away to type it'.[23]

Tselentis's role in the operation was again peripheral; he provided cover since he did not know how to use a gun and could not offer himself to drive the car that was used in the operation to block the way for Momferatos' Mercedes as he had never driven a car in his life. Tselentis remembers being puzzled at the time about the lack of training he was receiving from the group:

> I could not be used as a driver because I simply didn't know how to drive but nobody took me and taught me how. The same applied with guns. I had repeatedly asked to be taken some place to be shown how to use a gun

> but the answer I received was that there was not enough ammunition for training purposes. But I soon came to realize that special training was not needed because it was not necessary.[24]

Echoing the words of Eamon Collins, IRA man turned whistleblower, Tselentis explained that 'when a group of terrorists are determined and dedicated, when they devote their minds and energies to a task, they will succeed in doing things that seem to other people difficult to do. Shooting a man from a close range does not require training. It requires courage and conviction'.[25]

The Momferatos attack was deemed to be 'a success by the group, particularly because of the extensive media coverage that the 17N action received'. Tselentis also recalls reading a few days after the attack an article in *Eleftherotypia* which strongly argued that Momferatos had no connection with the CIA, an accusation levelled against him by the group in their proclamation. This was the first time that Tselentis realized that 'we might have got it wrong, our intelligence was wrong and we may have made a mistake. This got me thinking but I did not have the guts to share this with the other group members. I vividly remember feeling slightly awkward about the whole thing'.[26]

The next attack in which Tselentis took part was the assassination of Dimitris Angelopoulos, leading industrialist and chairman of the Halivourgiki steel company, in 1986. Angelopoulos, aged seventy-nine, had played a prominent role in Greece's steel industry and Halivourgiki, which he founded in the early 1950s, accounted at the time for 60 per cent of the country's steel production. Angelopoulos, 17N said, was targeted because, like a typical big Greek capitalist, while he deliberately let his state-aided Greek business go bankrupt, he smuggled out massive funds to make investments abroad. Referring to the Angelopoulos attack, Tselentis said that:

> thanks to the Greek media, there has been a great deal of inaccuracies, myths and innuendo and fairy tales regarding this operation and the selection of targets. In principle, targets were selected on the basis of what they represented and what they symbolized. That said, when the most symbolically appropriate target could not be selected because of the operational difficulties it posed, easier targets, somewhat inevitably, had to be selected. For instance, we had always wanted to go for [shipping magnate] Vardis Vardinoyiannis but during the time I was in 17N it was not logistically possible given his security and the armour-plated cars in which he was

driven around. [17N eventually did launch in 1992 a multi-rocket attack against the shipping magnate who miraculously escaped death]. Angelopoulos had the misfortune to like walking and that made him a far easier target than say Tsatsos, President of AGET, who may have been a symbolically stronger and better target but operationally a more difficult one given the special security precautions he was taking. Sometimes, Angelopoulos would choose to walk rather than go by car and this is why he was selected. He made an easy target.[27]

Walking Away from 17N

Towards the end of 1987, Tselentis felt that he could no longer justify 17N's activities, nor his direct role in those activities, and became disillusioned. For the first time in his 17N career he began to ask himself not only whether he should personally continue to be a member of the group but also whether the armed struggle itself was worth continuing. 'Running rapidly out of enthusiasm' and seriously alarmed by the degeneration of the group's campaign, Tselentis said that a point was reached when:

> it became very obvious that our actions and particularly our communiqués did not have the impact I had hoped they would. I could see that our initiatives were, in fact, distancing us from solutions instead of bringing us closer to them. I could also see society changing whereas we, myself and the other group members, were stuck in the past. My biggest problem, however, was that I could no longer comprehend the possessiveness on the part of some members for constant violent activity. This, in the language of the left, is called militarism. There was, in other words, a need for violent activity being carried out constantly but for no objective reason. I could also see no change or improvement in people's ways and attitudes. When I shared that with Koufodinas, he argued that making its members better was not among the aims of the organization. It was up to the individuals themselves, he said. My complaints over the necessity and regularity of our actions led to ill-feelings between myself and the rest of the group and that became obvious when they stopped asking me to take part in operations. The other problem I had was that as a member of this group, I had no private life. I couldn't start a family. I had to be secretive and constantly hiding and it came to a point when I realize that the whole thing was wrong. It had no potential and there was no way out. I kept seeing the group going for targets that, to me at least, made no sense. I couldn't understand why somebody's life had to be taken when a different type of action or the release of a communiqué would have achieved the same.[28]

Tselentis knew he was at a turning point. He began to reflect on his time to date in 17N and:

> reached the decision that I could no longer take part in such activities. When I talked openly to Koufodinas and informed him of my decision, he posed no objections whatsoever. Nor did he try to dissuade me by mentioning any [tacit] parts of any bargain that I was meant to keep... And no member from the group threatened me because of my decision to leave. As a matter of fact, I think that they felt relieved when I said that I wanted to leave the group as there had been disagreements and I would argue with them about aspects of the group's direction. I felt no fear when I decided to leave. In fact, I felt more fear when entering the group because of the personal sacrifices I would have to make. I became a member of the group and left from it fully conscious of what I was doing. From autumn '88 onwards, I never saw or tried to see anybody from the group and nor did they see me.[29]

What happens after disengagement, in terms of creating an identity that takes into account a previous role, is also an integral part of the role exit. After leaving the organization, Tselentis tried to make a new start, 'become a different person'.[30] Wrestling with himself because of his past, he tried to 'expiate for all the things' he had done:

> I tried becoming a model citizen, trying to help to the degree I was able to all the people around me who could do with my help. I joined the army, I honoured my superior officers and did not, for a second, abuse the confidence and trust they showed in me. I knew where I was, how I was and what I needed to do. I got married, got a job and tried to start again, tried to resume a normal life.[31]

Tselentis also tried to explain why, 'in spite of the fact that [he] disagreed with all this and could see that it was going nowhere', he still did not go to the police. 'There can be only one answer to this', he said. 'A member of such a group is a conscious member. He fervently believes that what he does is the right thing, is morally accepted. He feels, in many ways, that part of society condones his stance'.[32] To Tselentis it was clear that 'you don't betray people who are willing to sacrifice their lives for what they believe in even if you have come to disagree with them'.[33] The 17N *pentito* took his argument further by saying that it was one thing to disagree with comrades who pursued unrealisable goals by means of unrealistic strategies and another to give them in to 'police authorities whose methods and tactics, as everybody knows, have never inspired popular confidence'.[34] Tselentis did not avoid discussing the crucial issue of morality. To the question of how could he be perfectly willing to participate in assassinations of people but not find the courage to bring a solution to that problem, Tselentis's one-word reply was: 'cowardice'.[35]

Political violence, like those who use it, is complex but not indecipherable. If we want to understand the development of a terrorist from the time he enters a group to the time he decides to disengage and to further understand the reasons behind such decisions then we must pay attention not only to the individual but also to the individual's primary community of family, friends and country. Tselentis explained that the practice of armed struggle was deeply embedded in a national fabric of struggle, sacrifice and resistance. 'There was a history for us to follow', he argued, and these deep ideological structures and core elements were being carried in collective memory. Prescribing violence as a historically justified response to political oppression, Tselentis said that somebody like him:

> does what he does because he believes it is morally necessary and the right thing to do. But the key question here is: why does one reach that point? In this country where we live, a long history of struggle and sacrifice exists. Our country has experienced injustice which continues to this day. I lived in times when I felt the injustice all around me, when I felt that human life did not count for much. This is something that makes you want to put a stop to injustices. And this is what makes you take up arms using one form of injustice in order to stop another. It is not a question of giving justice. It is more of a question of showing people that you believe that injustice can be stopped, otherwise it will never stop.[36]

For Tselentis and his 17N comrades armed struggle had become the only possibility to avoid 'surrender'. To paraphrase French Action Directe militant Joelle Aubron, 17N's actions were 'born of the realization that a new kind of vanguard was needed in order to overthrow effectively all relationships that degrade, submit, subjugate and destroy men and women'.[37] 'With our actions', Tselentis explained:

> we wanted to show to those in power who were committing injustices that we could also do that. True, in practice, we ended up committing injustices ourselves but we considered that to be for a just and necessary cause. It was not a case of tit-for-tat, that is the people in power are doing injustices so we will do the same. We did what we did only because we wanted [Greek] society to see, understand and ultimately follow what we were doing.[38]

However, as time went on, the group turned in on itself, exaggerated its achievements and translated failures and misunderstandings as progress. In Tselentis's view, the decreasing contact with ordinary people and ordinary life and the constant preoccupation with the use of violence widened the gap between the group and the rest of society. As group members increasingly sought clandestinity either from necessity or from tactical choice, they became more abstracted and removed from practical reality. At the same time, as Tselentis explained, 'the fact that the police were incapable of getting even close to us gave us a sense of invincibility and power. But, sadly, power in all of its forms and manifestations can only result in arrogance and decadence and that is what infected the group in the end'.[39]

'A Process of Constant Personal and Political Transformation'

Red Brigades *pentito* Antonio Savasta would justify his 'penitence' in these terms:

> The necessity and the inevitability of the armed struggle represented our bet with history. Well, we lost that bet, and our isolation and defeat are the price for having defined reality by abstract theories which oversimplified it, for having concentrated the social reasons for change in a instrument unable to express it.[40]

Tselentis, like Savasta, began his terrorist career as a metropolitan guerrilla with a vision of politics thoroughly conditioned by romanticized concepts of sacrifice and death, but as the use and degree of fanaticism and violence increased he became 'spiritually tired'. 'I left the organization', Tselentis said:

> because I did not receive the ideological education that I expected to receive from a left-wing political organization. And to be more specific, what I had hoped was that certain people within the group would initiate certain processes that would improve the quality of the group members as people. This was what I expected from [group leaders] Koufodinas and Giotopoulos and this was one of the reasons why I joined the group in the first place.[41]

Throughout the group's trial, Tselentis challenged Koufodinas's most insistent position, which was that 17N's armed struggle was merely defensive:

> The only thing I can say is that this is not the way. And such practices lead to tragic results. The group members get cut off from society, take decisions

> outside society and their very own existence inside conspiratorial organizations has tragic consequences not only for society but also for themselves... Beyond their tragic victims, they are tragic victims themselves.[42]

Not surprisingly, Koufodinas admonished his 'former fighter and former friend, for choosing to go down the path of collaboration'. 'Patroklos Tselentis', said Koufodinas:

> found himself at the hands of the institutions he fought against when in 17N, but has now come to accept and support them. He decided to collaborate, to tell what these agencies want him to say, to hurt and slander the group and its members. However, he will soon discover that after choosing the path of collaboration, there is no turning back. After he has said whatever he thinks he needs to say that can be of benefit to him, after he speaks damagingly against all his co-defendants, after he has distorted the truth and defamed the organization, they will force him to lie even more before abandoning him like a used lemon rind to face up to society's contempt.[43]

Like his Italian Red Brigades comrade and counterpart Renato Curcio, Koufodinas also refused to give evidence within and outside of the court. Curcio's line of defence was: 'I am content with myself, with what I am, with what I have been',[44] while Koufodinas was somewhat similar: 'I won't do what you would want to do. I won't even bother entering your logic. Our morality does not accept logics of cooperation and squealing.'[45] Tselentis, on the other hand, choosing not to fall into the guerrilla hero/traitor dichotomy, came to accept that an armed minority could not command popular support nor affect social reality. As one of Tselentis's defence lawyers put it:

> Tselentis's understanding of the "enemy" has evolved. He has reconsidered the whole ideology of martyrdom of the armed struggle that nourished him throughout all the early years. Tselentis's repentance and rejection of revolutionary activism does not stem from his innocence but from a willingness to problematise the entire sense of 17N's modus operandi, and a willingness to engage himself fully in a process of constant personal and political transformation.[46]

Sotiris Kondylis

Sotiris Kondylis was the last suspected 17N member to be arrested, on 1 August 2002. He faced eighteen charges, including accessory in the assassination of Turkish diplomat Omer Haluk Sipahioglu in 1994 and the rocket attack on the US embassy in Athens in 1996, and simple complicity on three counts of attempted murder against police officers in a 1991 shootout with police in the central district of Sepolia. Unlike Tselentis, Kondylis did not become a *pentito*. He saw himself as a *dissociati* terrorist, as someone who dissociated himself from the armed struggle and the practice of violence for political ends. Known to other 17N members by the *nom de guerre* Aris, Kondylis joined the group in 1990 soon after Savvas Xiros's brother Christodoulos brought him into contact with Koufodinas. Kondylis was the only one of the 17N members to have had a long and public involvement in political movements. A trade unionist in the Amstel brewery where he worked since 1982, Tselentis initially joined the Greek Communist Party (KKE) but drifted to far-left organizations in the late 1980s once he was expelled from KKE due to political disagreements. In the 1990 general election, Kondylis ran a failed campaign for a parliamentary seat on an extreme-leftist ticket with Neo Aristero Revma in his home region of Evrytania in Central Greece, and was also an unsuccessful candidate in the eastern Athens district of Vyronas for a seat in the local city council at the October 1998 local elections.

Becoming Involved

Kondylis's actual involvement in the group was characterized by a very gradual progression. In reflecting upon his initial involvement in 17N, Kondylis points to having a strong awareness of unfolding social and political events at the start of the 1990s within and outside Greece:

> It was a very critical period. A new authoritarian [conservative] government had come to power launching a sustained assault against the labour force and the public sector via numerous privatizations of hitherto state-controlled industries. Violent student marches and political mobilizations were an everyday occurrence. There was the Yugoslav civil war raging on our doorstep, while at the same time Turkey was raising the stakes with regards to the Kurdish conflict and a year later, after forty years a coalition of nations attack another country on the pretext of the Iraqi invasion of Kuwait. My personal standpoint was that things were moving backwards instead of forwards, revisiting ugly past experiences.[47]

Kondylis was one of the hundreds of people who began at the time experimenting in radical politics, taking part in political seminars, marches, demonstrations and street battles with the police. Kondylis kept going to marches and became friendly with Christodoulos Xiros, who soon introduced him to Koufodinas. The idea of political violence began to work its way into Kondylis mind after having numerous political discussions with Xiros and Koufodinas who, clearly radicalized, seemed determined to turn to revolutionary militancy. 'The more conversations I had with them', Kondylis recalls:

> the more obvious it became that they wanted to use violent methods. Violence for me at that time went as far as screaming slogans during marches and clashing with the police. In fact during my time in the KNE [youth section of KKE] none of us threw rocks or Molotov cocktails at demonstrations—that for me was violence. We kept meeting to discuss what was happening, then Savvas [Xiros] joined in [who Kondylis did not know until the day of his arrest was Christodoulos's brother] and I soon realized what they had in mind when they said that we needed to respond with violence. I specifically asked if they were part of an existing group and they said that they weren't. Obviously, it never crossed my mind that the people I was joining to launch violent actions with were in any way connected to 17N. If there was any link to any other group, I thought to myself, it was likely to be some group from the Eksarcheia area [a neighborhood in downtown Athens frequented by leftists and anarchists]. Anyway, I agreed to go ahead.[48]

The Sepolia Incident

In November 1991 the Greek police came face to face with a 17N commando unit in Sepolia district, a mile away from the centre of Athens, but a combination of amateurism and panic allowed the terrorists to escape, leaving behind four wounded policemen. The shootout took place around midnight when a police patrol spotted three men trying to steal a Toyota minivan. The two police officers left their automatic weapons in the patrol car as they jumped out to arrest the suspects. But within seconds a fourth commando emerged from a parked car and opened fire with a pistol. Two more patrol cars were quickly on the scene, but were met with a barrage of hand grenades as the four 17N commandos made their getaway in a commandeered taxi.

The Sepolia incident was the first operation in which Kondylis took part. He recalled being nervous because nobody had mentioned to him anything about the plan or the target until a few hours before the operation:

> When we finally reached the target, Koufodinas handed us gloves and guns and it was only then realized that things were serious. When I said to them that we were only going to steal a van, why the need for guns, Koufodinas's reply was: Just in case something goes wrong. We don't carry guns to kill, he said.[49]

The Greek newspapers were full of reports the following days connecting the incident to 17N but Kondylis could still not bring himself to accept that he had become part of the group. 'Despite the media coverage, I did not give it much notice primarily because of Christodoulos's regular involvement in marches and skirmishes with the police—the risk of him being arrested was high.'[50] However, reality did sink in for Kondylis when Greek media reports confirmed that police ballistics tests pointed to 17N. 'It was weeks after the operation when we all got together and I was told who they really were.' When he protested for being kept in the dark all this time, it was explained to him that this was standard 17N procedure:

> Koufodinas said to me that for security reasons the approach to people who were keen and the group was interested in them joining had to and needed to be indirect. He also explained that if they were to reveal right from the beginning that they were 17N, the chances were that I would have said no and wouldn't have joined. For there were many rumours and conspiracy theories circulating about the organization at the time. Anyway, I accepted Koufodinas's explanations and assurances that they were who they said they were and nothing else.[51]

Should I Stay or Should I Go?

Conversion to violence requires a specific redefinition of reality, which the individual arrives at by adopting new beliefs and values. Unlike Tselentis, who took to the idea of becoming a 17N member almost instantly, Kondylis, perhaps because of the strongly emotional experience at Sepolia, remained undecided and took considerable time to decide whether or not to cross the Rubicon of 17N violence. Eventually, at the beginning of 1994, Kondylis, after numerous meetings and discussions with Koufodinas and Christodoulos Xiros, decided to join the group. He recalled having a meeting with Koufodinas where the group's operational leader said to him that 'it was time to choose whether to side with 17N or with the left'.[52] Kondylis recalls that he felt 'no pressure' to make up his mind:

> After a series of conversations I said to them: yes I want to join in. I really wanted to see for myself what this group was about; how it operated; who were the people behind it. It is a bit of a paradox, I know, because the group had been active for almost two decades and until I got into contact with them in '91, I never felt the need to seek involvement with a group such as 17N. I must say that it [17N] never touched me as a group. In fact, I hadn't even bothered to read the group proclamations and I had to go find a book that had them collected to see what the group's political positions were. What does the group say and think. To be honest, what I read wasn't anything special, anything different from what was already being discussed within the left circles and the parties, regardless of the fact that nothing of those discussed was ever put into practice.[53]

Kondylis's first proper involvement in a 17N operation came in July 1994 when the group ambushed senior Turkish diplomat Omer Haluk Sipahioglou outside his home The three-man squad pumped six bullets into Sipahioglou and drove away casually into the morning traffic. In a ferociously worded communiqué that was left on the scene and was signed '17 November—Theofilos Georgiadis Commando', 17N attacked the Turkish government for practising ethnic cleansing against the Kurds and the Greek-Cypriot community in occupied northern Cyprus. Speaking about the operation and his role in the attack, Tselentis explained that Theofilos Georgiadis was a Cypriot human rights activist who, the group believed, was assassinated in March 1994 in Nicosia by the MIT Turkish secret service for his pro-Kurdish political activities. 'We had to respond to the Georgiadis murder. Moreover, the Turkish government had, at the time, intensified its offensive against the Kurds burning down up to 2,700 Kurdish villages creating thousands of refugees.'[54] Kondylis's role in the Sipahioglou operation was to stay close to the getaway car and provide cover. Kondylis recalls the almost cinematic story of how the plan from going to check Sipahioglou's car route to the Turkish embassy quickly turned into on-the-spot full-blown assassination attack:

> That morning, the plan was to simply go and check the area—or at least this is what I was told. Once we got there, I stayed by the car close to a kiosk while Savvas [Xiros] and Koufodinas went and before five minutes had elapsed I heard gunshots and before I realized what was happening I saw Koufodinas and Savvas immediately behind him coming back towards the car with Savvas saying: let's go—the job is done. I was rather puzzled by the whole thing because this was the first operation I had taken part in and it looked totally disorganised. When I did raise this, I was told that an

> opportunity presented itself and it was decided that the operation could be done there and then.[55]

The next attack in which Kondylis took part was an IRA-style mortar attack against the American Embassy in Athens in February 1996, soon after the Imia incident, when Greece and Turkey almost went to war over the Aegean islet of Imia and it was only the intervention of US President Clinton and his Assistant Secretary of State Richard Holbrooke that actually prevented armed conflict between the two NATO allies. 17N's view, in the words of Kondylis, was that 'the long-standing animosity between Greece and Turkey did not actually serve the interests of either the Greek or the Turkish people and the conflict had been engineered by the Americans whose main priority is to control the region, sell their arms and protect their own regional interests'.[56] Kondylis's role in what was going to be his last operation was peripheral, providing cover as Koufodinas and Xiros launched the operation which, incidentally, failed disastrously as the rocket rammed into a security wall and exploded 100 meters from the embassy compound.

Exit

The rocket attack against the US embassy in Athens was to be Kondylis's last operation for the group. Like every other aspect of Kondylis's involvement with 17N his experiences of disengagement and withdrawal were neither simple nor straightforward. Soon after the operation Kondylis's father fell seriously ill. After several months of hospitalization, Kondylis took his ill father home because 'there wasn't anything more they could at the hospital'.[57] It seems that his father's illness was for Kondylis the tipping point; it was the singular event that catalyzed his disengagement from the group. 'All this time', he explained, during my father's illness:

> I had time to think things through, to reflect, and reached the conclusion that it was no longer necessary to continue with armed action as it made no sense. Lots of changes were taking place in the country, there was a new socialist modernizing government that promised reforms and transparency, the country was now making progress as a solid part of the EU, the American President [Bill Clinton] had apologized during his visit to Athens for past wrongs, Athens was to host the Olympic Games and I became convinced that the group's militant activity had to come to an end.[58]

Kondylis's s next step was to make his case to 17N's operational leader Koufodinas, who he thought was sharing similar views with regards to 17N's future:

> I spoke to him, we had a long talk about this, and we reached the conclusion that I could no longer help because of time constraints and my ideas. In fact, I sincerely believed that Koufodinas himself had similar views to mine at the time. He shared my doubts regarding the continuation of the group. My feeling was—I could have been wrong, of course—that he was asking the same questions I was asking "Where were we going? Where was he going?" In the end he stayed on but he should have left too. Anyway, we agreed to terminate our agreement and I returned to normality and my previous everyday life.[59]

'Guns Need Hands but They Also Need Ideas'

Analyzing the life histories of Patroklos Tselentis and Sotiris Kondylis offers valuable insights into the development of complex processes of involvement in and disengagement from 17N terrorism. The detail stemming from such testimonies provides a more complete picture of the group's internal dynamics and challenges a range of simplistic stereotypes, not only about the individuals involved in terrorism but also about the ways in which they make decisions and reflect on their experiences of being part of a terrorist organization. Posing the question of *how* individuals disengage from a terrorist group can be as illuminating as posing the question of *why* they do so. Ideological reasons, tactical disagreements, moral considerations, doubts about the rationale and future of armed struggle and the strain of life in the underground were the main factors that prompted Tselentis to turn away from terrorism. Tselentis's method of facilitating disengagement was the low-key, quiet withdrawal approach. He gradually made himself marginal to the group, taking less and less part in group activities, displaying a lack of interest in order to make the group lose interest in him. The 17N group leadership in turn, unlike the Red Brigades in Italy and the Red Army Faction in Germany, did not at any stage demand from Tselentis total and continued loyalty to the 'revolutionary community', nor did they attempt to control him through domination of his private life, and this made disengagement and exit relatively straightforward and devoid of emotional intensity.

Terrorists' political ideas always tend to reflect a given society's radical ideological currents and Tselentis, described by an anti-terrorism prosecutor as 'a man of extreme principles hesitantly held', did these things for specific reasons and principles.[60] It is not hard to see, given 17N's advancing militarism, why Tselentis came to accept that 17N's armed struggle, like BR's before them, was 'maintained and justified in the imaginations of those who practised it until the moment when reality intrudes on myth and gradually destroys it'.[61] Tselentis subscribed to the Greek state's repentance rules not simply because he rejected 'the practice of armed struggle' but because his repentance gave him 'a sense of freedom, that comes from the possibility to recollect your life using the normal logic for which murder is murder, wounding is wounding, a ferocious comrade is a ferocious man, and not a vanguard with a higher level of class consciousness'.[62]

Kondylis's case, on the other hand, brings out forcefully the fact that for certain individuals, to use the words of former Red Army Faction guerrilla Knut Folkerts, 'the choice of armed struggle—when everything is said and done—is first and foremost an existential decision to make'.[63] Political violence was not Kondylis's element, his natural habitat. However, his close proximity to violence, his particular childhood influences and his fascination with social upheaval influenced his awareness of unfolding political events, catalyzing his commitment and motivation in participating in terrorist groups. His account confirms the argument that although 'activists in armed groups preserve a political purpose, they also look in their surroundings for confirmation of their own choices'.[64] Kondylis may have inhabited the same world as those politically active individuals around him, and was moved by the same concerns, but the 17N *dissociati*, prompted by the desire for political commitment, moved from extremism to terrorism almost without realizing it. 'The moment you find yourself involved', he said, 'you've gone over the line. And once you've done that the entire thing goes much deeper than your personal participation in any particular action. You lose your way'.[65]

Kondylis turned out to be a paradigmatic 17N *dissociato*. As the word suggests, he dissociated himself from the armed struggle and the practice of violence for political ends, at the same time urging people not to take up the ways of violence. 17N, Kondylis acknowledged, had been defeated politically as well as ideologically. 'Guns needs hands but they also need ideas. If the ideas are not there, the guns won't work.'[66]

Terrorism in general, and Greek terrorism in particular, constitutes a great deal more than the sum of individual acts, but we need to have some understanding of the individual terrorist and the ways in which issues such as fellow group members, choice of targets and justification impact upon him or her. The reflections of both Tselentis and Kondylis are illuminating, for they not only bring us closer to understanding elements of the processes involved but also provide us with a more complete picture of the group's internal dynamics, organizational structure, membership, leadership, logistics and communications.

5

ETERNAL REVOLUTIONARY

CHRISTOS TSIGARIDAS AND THE REVOLUTIONARY POPULAR STRUGGLE (ELA)

On 29 April 1975 the history of Greek revolutionary terrorism began. Eight cars belonging to US servicemen at the military base of Elefsina were firebombed. A previously unknown group calling itself Revolutionary Popular Struggle or *Epanastatikos Laikos Agonas* (ELA) claimed responsibility for the attack. Believing in the violent overthrow of the capitalist state and in an ill-defined socialist Greek society based on the principles of Marxist-Leninist ideology, the group went on to carry out a systematic campaign of non-lethal, low-level bombings that lasted for two decades. Founded by left-wing activist Christos Kassimis, ELA viewed itself as part of the international revolutionary movement of the day, and therefore counted US imperialism, capitalism and fascism in all their various forms as its enemies. As a result, all ELA terrorist attacks were directed at symbolic material targets—ranging from US military and business facilities to EC and UN offices, foreign embassies and Greek government buildings—all of which represented one or more of these enemies. Despite its violent rhetoric, it soon became evident that, unlike 17N, ELA actions were primarily intended to publicise its political message rather than to cause bloodshed.[1] Through the regular publication of its underground journal *Andipliroforissi* (Counter Information) the group outlined its strategic priorities and communicated with its supporters and sympathisers and other like-minded groups of the revolutionary left.

Christos Tsigaridas joined ELA in 1976 through his connection to Kassimis, a year before the ELA founder was killed in a shootout with the police at an attempted terrorist strike at the AEG factory in Rendi, western Athens, where he was about to place an explosive device. The death of Kassimis must have caused organizational turmoil within the group, given that it took almost two years for ELA to resume its bombing campaign, and it is believed to have resulted in the withdrawal of a large number of members. It was at this critical juncture that Tsigaridas is believed to have taken up the reins.[2] Tsigaridas, however, steadfastly denied any leadership role during the ELA trial that followed that of 17N in 2004 in the same Korydallos high-security prison courtroom. Tsigaridas, a sixty-four-year old Athens architect at the time, denied any operational role in ELA's bombing campaign, claiming instead to have been in charge of ELA propaganda and the *Andipliroforissi* journal. Tsigaridas, the only one to have admitted group membership, insisted that he left ELA in 1990 'due to personal reasons' and refused to help incriminate his fellow-defendants—three men and a woman—whom he described as innocent victims of police persecution and vindictiveness.[3]

Formative Experiences

Christos Tsigaridas was born in 1935 in the village of Xylagani, 35 kilometres away from the city of Komotini in northeastern Greece. Tsigaridas never met his father, who died during the 1940–41 Greco-Italian War which marked the beginning of the Balkans campaign in the Second World War.[4] During the Nazi occupation of Greece, the family moved to Tsigaridas's grandfather's village of Biletsi, close to Trikala in north-western Thessaly, which remained under Greek guerrilla control. Tsigaridas's mother, who had lived until her twenties in Leningrad, became actively involved with the communist-led resistance movement of EAM/ELAS, the Greek People's Liberation Army, one of the largest and most impressive resistance movements in Nazi-occupied Europe.[5] After the war was over, in 1945, the Tsigaridas family moved to Athens. In the ideologically charged atmosphere of the Greek capital, Tsigaridas acquired the central beliefs of his political life. As the country descended into a full-scale civil war that greatly compounded the human suffering and material losses sustained during the Axis occupation, a state-organized campaign of mass political repression against the communist left was launched in the name of 'national security'.[6] The impact on Tsigaridas's way of thinking is revealed in his remark that:

> this period was for me a period of social and political coming of age. In Athens I saw my mother being called names such as 'bolshevik' and 'bandit' by her own mother. In the village, I saw the full consequences of monarcho-fascism upon proud, decent people who fought for freedom and national independence. Those labelled as *non-ethnikofrones* were not able to get even seasonal work. I saw young people with university degrees languishing in society's margins with no jobs. The prerequisite for a better life was to become an *ethnikofron*, or a law-abiding citizen and sign a written statement as confirmation. And it was the gendarmerie that would make or break people's lives.[7]

The tipping point for Tsigaridas came at the age of seventeen. Until then, as he conceded in court, 'even though I could see everything that was happening around me and in spite of my mother's interpretations, I wasn't, for some reason, able, or perhaps I didn't want, to connect to a central political message'.[8] The catalyst for Tsigaridas to 'wake up and realize what was actually happening', was a chance meeting with the widow and two children of the village teacher and communist who had been, according to Tsigaridas, murdered by a right-wing gang. 'She came to find me in the village square, gave me this notebook and said: "Take it, you're educated, you live in the capital, make the most of it in memory of my husband."' The notebook was essentially a letter to his family—full of love and compassion—explaining the reasons why he had to die for his beliefs. That letter and the teacher's brave stance—'one of the thousands of communists who proudly faced death for their political beliefs'—marked his character and his life.[9]

By the time Tsigaridas enrolled at the Athens Polytechnic, he had made revolutionary change the main plank of his political ideology. He read and reread in both Greek and English 'everything about Marxism' and became convinced that 'for the poverty, injustice, misery and barbarity I could see around me, there was an explanation, there was a cause and there was also a way out'.[10] The political and economic structure was offensive to young Tsigaridas: 'the existing capitalist exploitative state apparatus had to be smashed and it was the role of the working-class movement to bring about wholesale revolutionary change'.[11] In his first year at the Polytechnic, Tsigaridas joined the youth organization of the United Democratic Left (EDA), an alliance of a number of leftist groupings which stood as a front for the outlawed Greek Communist Party (KKE).[12] Tsigaridas also joined EDA's university newspaper *Panspoudastiki* as a political cartoonist and member of the editorial team. The future ELA militant spent the next few years leading an action-packed political existence. The *Panspoudastiki* editorial team, he recalled 'consisted of gifted young students who were fighting for the advancement of the student communist movement. We would spend days and nights, discussing and debating the great issues, and that matured me politically.'[13]

As EDA grew stronger, the exiled leaders of KKE began to view their EDA counterparts as a dangerous faction capable of developing their own political potential and thus challenging the legitimacy of their authority. The trench political warfare that followed between the 'interior' and 'exiled' party leaderships led to sectarianism and ideological confusion within the Greek communist left, opening the door for revolutionary radicalism. Hundreds of disillusioned defectors, Tsigaridas among them, felt that the communist left had not been sufficiently radical in its methods, aims and policies. They subsequently formed new breakaway groups, turning to themes and issues that the party establishment had chosen to ignore:

> worker's control and human self-emancipation, university authoritarianism, social hierarchy and the repressive mechanisms of political control.[14]
> Reflecting on internal divisions in Greece and abroad, Tsigaridas developed a corrosive disdain for communist party bosses, blaming them for:
> turning revolutionary parties into parties of the establishment. Parties that strive to find a tiny little position under the parliamentary sun. Parties that sell out the interests of the working people for their own particular political needs. Parties that weigh down the feet of the working popular movement. Parties that have replaced revolutionary strategy for the overthrow of capitalism with peaceful coexistence and the peaceful transition to socialism, sliding into opportunism.[15]

As in 1952, when the widow of the village teacher approached him, the 1967 military coup, when it came, seems to have marked a watershed moment in Tsigaridas's life. The events which led to the military junta had more to do with the army's distrust of the political establishment (the parliament and the palace) and less to do with the revolutionary threat posed by the fractured communist left. Looking back on the seven years of the military junta, Tsigaridas deplored the KKE's feeble resistance to the Colonels. As he recalled, 'it had become rather obvious at a much earlier stage than when it actually came that a junta, imposed by the foreign powers in collaboration with their domestic lackeys, was on its way'. But the image of 'leftists and communists, waiting with their suitcases ready for the secret police to knock on their door and take the road to political exile without being given the chance by the party to resist, to put up a fight', was shocking to him. The party, Tsigaridas argued, 'had put no mechanism in place that would absorb and organise those activists who were prepared to resist. There was nothing! It had all collapsed. Why would a party with such fighting history and tradition behind it not prepare for the imminent dictatorship and allow its organization to dissolve?'[16] For Tsigaridas, the lack of political resistance on the part of the KKE prior to and during the junta years and its subsequent acceptance of 'the farce that *metapolitefsi* was' represented its complete turnaround from a revolutionary movement to an establishment party.

The Metapolitefsi of 1974

Admittedly, the *metapolitefsi* of 1974, the transition from an authoritarian rule to a democratic constitutional order, was not the result of a clear and sharp break with the Colonels' regime, but the product of a whole range of compromises and negotiations between elite-level political actors and the military. More specifically, the end of the dictatorship and the surrender of power to a civilian government was neither the result of a military counter-coup in Athens nor a popular upheaval from below. Rather, it resulted from the 20 July Turkish invasion of northern Cyprus (38 per cent of the island) and the inability of the Colonels to handle the crisis and deal with a rapidly deteriorating military situation.

In Tsigaridas's view:

> the dictatorship was finished by the same powers which had imposed it in the first place; *metapolitefsi* was a cosmetic change imposed by the Americans and NATO as Andreas Papandreou had very perceptively pointed out, although he later "forgot" about this and many other things. But it was a change that ordinary Greek people did not see for what it was. The mainstream parties made certain that any popular scepticism was channelled to harmless for the system directions, while at the same time a new political establishment was created to run the capitalist socioeconomic system.[17]

Having acquired the mainstream left's support, the system, according to Tsigaridas, was 'the last bit in the puzzle for completing the political changeover, moving from a dictatorial to a parliamentary form of governance, whereby the rich are getting richer and the poor are getting poorer, no longer aided by the junta but by Parliament'.[18] In surveying the history of *metapolitefsi*, Tsigaridas made a point that has been made countless times before: that without any systematic purge, key sections of the state continued in the hands of the old, fascistic order.[19] Reflecting on the poor, cosmetic attempts at dejuntification or *apohountopoiisi*, Tsigaridas argued that the post-1974 regime:

> did everything it could to leave Greek people in no doubt that it helped to facilitate a dynastic about-turn, a real change within the elite political personnel of a capitalist state power. Apart from the junta leaders, all the key people that made up the junta state apparatus remained unpunished. Not even an elementary catharsis of the state mechanisms was attempted. All the appointees of, and collaborators with, the junta in state bureaucracy, the police apparatus, education and the judiciary remained untouched.[20]

For Tsigaridas, *metapolitefsi* may have been 'a dynastic change of regime', but at the same time, it produced new solidarities as it released:

> a massive social movement that felt suppressed and asphyxiated during the dictatorship years. There was a sharp growth of social movement organisations using forms of collective action, to make new demands and gain political space, that had not been seen for years. Of course, this movement had its contradictions and its limitations, which stemmed from the efforts of the mainstream left parties to push people back towards compliance and non-resistance.[21]

Metapolitefsi, as Tsigaridas pointed out, presented the Greek left with a new set of challenges, for it marked the return, 'in heightened form', of all the issues that had been festering since the 1960s, deepening the ever widening schism between the mainstream and anti-mainstream components of the left.[22] The issues were of an ideological, programmatic, tactical and organizational nature and dealt with questions such as:

> peaceful or revolutionary transition to socialism? Legal activity or a required mixture of legal and illegal activity? What was the role of revolutionary violence within the conditions of *metapolitefsi*? How to built an independent syndicalist movement? What relationship needs to be constructed between the revolutionary vanguard and the mass social movement?[23]

All these questions, Tsigaridas said, 'were then broken down to subquestions which would in turn stimulate theoretical discussions and political disagreements, intellectual and polemical debates in numerous action committees because one had to remember that besides the legal, parliamentary left, an entire revolutionary movement existed with its own factions, disputes, and power struggles'.[24] These action committees turned to controversial issues that the mainstream left ignored and gave people of different ages and different experiences the opportunity to share those experiences and to express their opinions on political matters of common concern. The action committee that Tsigaridas joined, where he would first meet his political mentor Kassimis, fulfilled two personal preconditions: 'it did not operate within narrow party-political parameters and it had no aspirations to develop into a political party'. As he explained, it was a committee that felt it had the duty to foster revolutionary consciousness and widen solidarity with all areas of society, particularly in factories, neighbourhoods and universities.

Meeting Christos Kassimis

Christos Kassimis was destined to become the leading theoretician of the Greek revolutionary movement, but he never fulfilled his destiny. He was shot through the head in October 1977 by the Athens police while attempting to firebomb the AEG factory in Piraeus to protest against a visit of the German Chancellor Helmut Schmidt. A soft-spoken and cultured revolutionary communist activist, Kassimis always led, according to Tsigaridas, from the front, through his example and presence. Belonging to the same action committee, Kassimis and Tsigaridas soon became friends and began to 'discuss the armed struggle'.[25] It is not difficult to imagine the impact of such conversations on Tsigaridas. As Tsigaridas recalled, 'after a month of talking, he [Kassimis] brought me ELA's manifesto *Yia tin anaptyxi tou Elllinikou Laikou kai Epanastatikou Kinimatos* [For the Development of the Greek Popular and Revolutionary Movement] and asked me to consider joining the group'.[26] Tsigaridas's conversion was not, however, instant. 'It took us six months', Tsigaridas recalled, 'to go through the whole document. We analyzed the text's every single paragraph, every single word. And after six months of discussions, having found myself in ideological, political and organizational agreement, I became a member of ELA.'[27] Organizationally, the group was not monolithic. It was comprised, as Tsigaridas explained, of 'different, horizontally linked autonomous parts, each of which was responsible for divergent tasks'.[28] Although compartmentalized, this organizational structure provided, according to Tsigaridas, 'collective functionality and ensured the smooth circulation of information and views across the group, encouraging at the same time the development of criticism and self-criticism among all group members'. Every member had a group contact and Tsigaridas's contact within ELA was Kassimis until his death in 1977.[29] 'During our meetings', Tsigaridas recalled, 'there would be an open discussion on group activity and other matters followed by personal views and criticisms, if I had any.'[30]

ELA's Physiognomy

Looking back on his early years with ELA and the radical politics of the mid-1970s, Tsigaridas said that ELA saw itself as a part of the Greek autonomist movement and sought to give shape to a politico-military formation within that movement. Having observed autonomist movements in neighbouring Italy and Germany, ELA leaders believed that there was potential for the more radical fringes within the movement to express discontent and radicalize Greece's political situation. ELA tried setting up a network structure of autonomist support that would 'cut through the correct choice of targets and type of actions' and strengthen the armed initiative against the regime.[31] At a deeper level, the autonomist movement articulated social antagonisms and frustrations felt inside the movement for its betrayal by the reformist left'.[32] The autonomists, Tsigaridas said, had consciously broken off links not only with the communist left and its unions for their complicity with the establishment but also with the various new extra-parliamentary leftist groups which they considered the guard dogs of democratic 'legality'.[33] The autonomist movement, Tsigaridas further explained, 'was more than an attack against the socio-ideological consensus and much more than a critique against the left, and the left of the left. It was a reflection of the potential for the birth and development of a proletarian movement.'[34]

ELA believed it had a role to play. ELA, Tsigaridas said, was 'a revolutionary communist organization that saw it as its duty to contribute to the development of the popular movement'.[35] ELA implicitly believed that 'if revolutionary change was to take place in Greek society', the group had to 'pursue and cultivate a more direct relationship with the movement.'[36] In order to do that, the group had to take a three step approach. The first step was for the group to 'refresh', via its military activity 'society's memory on the need for revolutionary violence'.[37] Step two would involve 'the creation of several simultaneous guerrilla fronts which ELA would avoid absorbing by showing them the necessary respect and sensitivity for their different ideologico-political positions'.[38] Whatever differences there were, the group leadership was certain they would be resolved when it had become apparent who the real, common enemy was.[39] Step three involved the task of 'building an autonomist mass movement' whose chief aim would be to maintain ongoing politico-military activity against the regime.[40] A movement such as this would ultimately serve as 'a funnel' where political activism and armed militancy could be linked closely and the two levels of discourse would be complementary to each other.[41]

ELA, Tsigaridas clarified, was 'totally opposed to the theory of stages as a revolutionary tactic and strategy'.[42] Following the Red Brigadist view, violence was axiomatic to the model of the socialist revolution ELA wished to achieve. There was, in fact, 'a whole series of cultural models which indicated that any major change in history had always passed through vicious conflict between those defending the old social order and those wanting to impose the new'.[43] In the eyes of ELA, the capitalist regime would be overthrown by 'a popular revolutionary militant movement which would draw support and recruits from the exploited and suppressed masses'. This conflagration that would eventually lead to 'the total and permanent destruction of the capitalist society' would be 'a long and hard struggle'. The implication was that conditions were never going to be favourable and a belief in the ability of the revolutionary popular movement to persevere and show strength and commitment to the cause in the face of adversity was paramount. Consolidating everyday political resistance 'in every situation, at every level, on all fronts of social life' was fundamental.

Organizationally, ELA rejected hierarchy and leadership. 'There was no scope', Tsigaridas emphasized, 'for playing the boss'.[44] The group founders subdivided the organization into departments and the departments into cells, each unit operating independently from the others to ensure security and prevent infiltration. Regarding ELA's 'political practices', the group, Tsigaridas said, was organized along four axes: 1) Propaganda/counter-information; 2) Participation in the mass movement; 3) Revolutionary violence and 4) Political initiatives. A multilevelled and multi-dimensional propaganda was essential 'not for reasons of self-publicity and self-promotion but to expose everything that state mechanisms and the regime's mass media outlets hid, distorted and obfuscated'. ELA participation in the mass movement was equally important as it opened up 'possibilities for industrial protest and dissent in the factories, labour agitation and radicalization of the mainstream movement'. Revolutionary violence would not merely aim at 'eradicating the regime's monopoly of violence but at the same time would sharpen the reflections and class consciousness of the oppressed and exploited, rearming them with the desire to take part in waging war against capital'. Finally, political initiatives were crucial for 'the development of class conflict in every social sphere and space and for ripping holes in the reformism that poisons and paralyzes peoples' consciousness'.[45]

ELA's central concept concerned the role of the masses in the revolution and the establishment of a socialist society. The group used propaganda and factory management targets to increase tension between strikers and employers since it believed that conditions in the workplace were designed by the capitalist bosses to dehumanize and isolate the working class population. Wishing to provide a strong existential impetus behind the movement, ELA members became actively involved in 'worker mobilizations and neighbourhood assemblies in order to nourish aversion to party reformism and push initiatives in a class-based direction'. Each of them, Tsigaridas recalled, 'did political work in factories and the community, writing up political texts, distributing coupons, connecting workers from other factories, organizing music festivals, even paying fines which activists had incurred in courts'. ELA firmly believed that the working class movement had been very poorly served by the communist KKE. Far from being prime agents of the dissemination of radical value systems, ELA believed that KKE party leaders had turned themselves into opponents of any such system 'weaning organized labour and the working class away from anything that could be called socialist revolutionary consciousness'.[46]

ELA's central goal, according to Tsigaridas, was to establish a political line that would facilitate revolutionary unity and consciousness inside the working class movement. As such, the group firmly believed that authentic revolution could be consciously constructed through workers' actions, ELA members in their factory and community work that tried to link revolutionary radicalism to concrete social transformations. At the same time, they fed the view 'that the workers' revolution was underway and direct action was credible', endorsing a variety of methods. ELA factory agitation sought to encourage greater worker militancy during industrial action. The group provoked, for instance, confrontations with supervisory personnel, labour unionists and strikebreakers. It also supported militant committees which in turn organized counter-violence against security personnel and the police forces during demonstrations.

The Andipliroforissi *Journal*

ELA also used an underground publication, namely *Andipliroforissi* (Counter-information). The journal, which Tsigaridas edited for most of his ELA career, became a propaganda channel for the group to outline its politico-military strategy and communicate with its supporters, sympathizers and other like-minded groups of the revolutionary left. *Andipliroforissi* was distributed through some clandestine channels and the state-run postal service. The first issue came out shortly after ELA's debut attack in Elefsina, but Tsigaridas has argued in court that contrary to popular belief, *Andipliroforissi* was not ELA's own journal. It was 'a mass revolutionary publication produced by an editorial committee, and involved a great number of people given the huge amount of work that was required for every issue of the journal'. Although he has never admitted it for reasons that have possibly more to do with conspiratorial rules and less with modesty, Tsigaridas explained that the manner in which *Andipliroforissi* was produced was 'a true reflection of the way ELA saw itself and the movement'. ELA, Tsigaridas said, never wished to become a party and never wanted to become the centre of the movement'.

Tsigaridas's involvement with ELA and *Andipliroforissi* may have ended in 1989 but the very last issue of the journal was published in May 1990. Entitled 'Disinformation, Propaganda and Ideological Agitation', the issue was twenty-three closely typed pages long and was of particular interest because ELA announced its alliance with the Revolutionary Organization 1 May. It will never be known what impact Tsigaridas's exit had on the group's strategic orientation but the partnership with 1 May was to have a dramatic effect on ELA operational strategy. On 26 February 1992, after almost eighteen years of bloodless bombings, the group suddenly escalated to lethal attacks. In a joint operation with 1 May, ELA detonated a remote-controlled device against a Greek police bus causing serious injuries to eighteen MAT riot policemen. Before February 1992, ELA had never used remote-detonated devices, never expanded its tactics beyond low-level bombings and never attempted to cause casualties.

Tsigaridas has never publicly commented on the operational departure of the group nor on the joint venture between ELA and 1 May which came to an end in 1995. Speaking of ELA's hundreds of non-lethal, low-level bombings, Tsigaridas said that they were:

> aimed at symbolic material targets and every single one of them linked to existing social problems. No attack ever took place for show or for group self-promotion. ELA always offered proper justification of its actions via the attack communiqués it released and always took the necessary precautions to avoid human casualties.

Tsigaridas argued that the approach ELA had chosen had nothing to with morality. It was both 'a conscious political and tactical decision on the part of the group to try and close the gap between what an organized revolutionary force could achieve with what a group of fighters or even the popular movement itself could do'. ELA always intended not to create an audience by its actions but worked instead towards the development of revolutionary counter-violence and to make it custom and practice for Greek society. ELA actions were not aimed, Tsigaridas said, at causing material damage to the targets themselves but at sending a message of resistance, to energize and push the people, the working class and youth towards the direction of dynamic resistance without necessarily using the same means that ELA used, but with all the available forms of popular counter-violence.[47]

Accepting Full Responsibility

Tsigaridas exited ELA in 1989. His decision to leave the organization coincided with the exit of his own contact who, having also decided to leave the group for 'personal reasons', offered to arrange a meeting with his replacement. Tsigaridas did not immediately object but—as he must have been seriously thinking about making an exit—he said that the organization should no longer consider him active if he failed to make that meeting. Tsigaridas did not go to the next meeting and never had any further contact with the group. In 2003, when Tsigaridas was arrested at his home in the wealthy suburb of Psychiko and jailed on felony charges for belonging to a terrorist group, he accepted without delay the full 'political responsibility' of his ELA membership. Despite suffering from lung cancer at the time, Tsigaridas said that it was inconceivable for him not to have done so. ELA, he said, was 'part of my personal and revolutionary trajectory and I am proud of it'.[48]

Reflecting upon the significance of his arrest, which came at a time of a major counter-terrorist drive on the part of the Greek state, with the entire 17N group already behind bars, Tsigaridas said he was determined to take the political responsibility irrespective of what incriminating evidence the security services had on him or 'whatever evidence they were going to fabricate' in order to incriminate him.[49] Having realized that time was up and that 'the end of the road had been reached', Tsigaridas informed his family of his decision—'the product of a tortuous internal process'—and of what was to follow. His decision to take responsibility was not, he said:

> an impulsive one nor was it a pretentious one. It was the grown-up decision to take, for take, for each individual is entitled to act according to his moral values. And my moral values, the way in which I see the duties of a communist, determined the way in which I acted. It is self-explanatory why I did what I did.[50]

Tsigaridas went further to say there was more at stake than his personal freedom and pride. Following the arrests of 17N and ELA members, Tsigaridas recollected, there was an atmosphere of counter-terrorism hysteria but also an attempt by the state and its security agencies to discredit the armed revolutionary organizations in particular, and the revolutionary left in general. Revolutionary organizations were presented as mafia gangs committing crimes against the people, and their members as gangsters. This being so, Tsigaridas explained, 'my conscience would simply not allow me to sit there and do nothing in defending the revolutionary honour of my group, ELA'. There had to be 'a response to all the constant media attacks, to the books and the mythical imaginings of authors on the payroll of the anti-terrorist police'. At the same time, Tsigaridas said, ELA had to send a message to the people that were involved or had been involved with the group and to the wider revolutionary circles that ELA members do not leave their organization undefended.

In Tsigaridas's eyes there was no alternative:

> I had previously thought about it long and hard and had come to the conclusion that if it ever came to my arrest then I would have no choice but to

accept political responsibility in order to defend the history of the group in public and make sure that the memory and sacrifice of its murdered members like Kassimis were not dishonoured and tainted. After half a century of political activity as a communist I felt it as my duty and acted as such.

Revolutionary Violence in the Time of 'Democracy'

Like Koufodinas, 17N's chief organizer, Tsigaridas used his court testimony to defend his group's violent actions by placing them in the political and historical context of the period. In the very same courtroom, Koufodinas had embraced the view that Greece's 'self-negating democracy' necessitated exactly the type of political violence 17N had undertaken. ELA's theoretician scathingly criticized every stage of Greece's post-1974 political discourse, arguing that a democracy that did not confront the misdeeds and miscreants of the past was 'a democracy perpetually flawed'.

Everywhere Tsigaridas looked he saw stagnation, disproportion and decline. Showing typical wit and dramatizing his points, Tsigaridas said:

> we often hear people wondering why there is revolutionary violence in the time of democracy, given that in a democracy we are free and that it is the popular will that should prevail. And given also that in a democracy it is the people who choose their leaders, elect and deselect their governments. It should be straightforward: for those who want to advance a political view, all they have to do is create a political party, compete in elections and seek the popular vote. If the people decide not to support them then they will have to respect the popular verdict. But people who pose such questions would seem to have landed from a different planet. But since they are residents of the planet Earth, as I am, as we all are, they can only be hypocrites.[51]

Surveying the political discourse of the past forty years, Tsigaridas lambasted Greek democracy, locating the scope and intensity of politicized discontent and alienations in the economic system, class structure and political institutions. He said he belonged to an age in which 'the profits of the industrialists kept getting bigger with every year that passes whereas the workers kept getting poorer'. Running from top to bottom, he added, the deep polarizations in Greece's inequality-riven society were constant mental reminders of capitalist exploitation and corporate greed. 'What kind of democracy is it', he rhetorically asked, 'when every year hundreds of workers die in industrial "accidents", lose hands and limbs or die prematurely from unacceptable working conditions?'[52] The privatization of health care provision was another issue that Tsigaridas touched upon, saying that Greece's national health care system was a disgrace, with collapsing hospitals, shambolic services and the economically weak, who could not afford private health insurance, left with nothing more than their democratic right to die, since their national health insurance amounted to nothing. Education was another issue Tsigaridas raised. The Greek educational system, he argued, not only reproduced the ideology of the dominant class but was also designed to 'produce graduates with limited expertise and knowledge who can be manipulated by the multinational companies and big capital'. The central narrative that prevails, he added:

> is that if you do not become a doctor or a lawyer or an engineer you will be socially inferior and financially insecure. This explains why huge amounts of Greek household budgets are being spent on shadow education (private lessons and tuitions) in order to meet the requirements of the fierce competition for a university place. In other words, a big chunk of Greece's GDP that belongs to the public is being given to the private sector. Private education, private insurance, private health care.[53]

Considerable attention was also paid by Tsigaridas to police violence and brutality. The ELA theoretician deplored the excessive use of force by the Greek state security forces and the lack of accountability for an entrenched pattern of serious human rights violations by law enforcement officials, which included excessive use of force, torture and other ill-treatment, and the misuse of firearms. In 'democracy' the 'accidental firing' of police guns which 'always happen to be killing young unarmed demonstrators, immigrants, drug addicts, gypsies or anybody else on the margins is acceptable and non-punishable'. In trying to rebut the claim that the police had a duty to uphold public order, particularly when attacked with bottles, rocks, and Molotov cocktails, Tsigaridas cited a Greek parliamentarian's statistic which showed civilian deaths amounted to seventy over recent years. In this context, Tsigaridas also raised the subject of what he called regular 'unjust and prefabricated persecutions' of known far-left activists and 'social fighters' by the state security mechanisms. There was a very long list, Tsigaridas said, of such people. Like Yiannis Serifis and Kostas Balafas and Epaminondas Skyftoulis, 'who have been at some point arrested, imprisoned, tried and condemned for serious crimes only for them to be eventually cleared, absolved and finally acquitted. But then again, this is our democracy and those who dare confront it, get to be characterised as criminal personalities.'[54]

The Central Dilemma of the Age: 'Communism or Barbarism?'

Tsigaridas was an ideologue of unshakeable beliefs. Having adopted at an early age a definite ideology that gave him a strong motivation to fight, his political analysis underwent development but it never substantially changed.[55] Seeing the world through the prism of certain basic ideas, Tsigaridas, like many twentieth-century revolutionary intellectuals before him, 'blinkered himself to the merits of alternative options'.[56] From the moment he turned to revolutionary militancy to the moment he was arrested and found himself in court, he never abandoned the unrealistic agenda he had set for himself and the ELA group. 'If you are wondering to what extent I have repented', Tsigaridas told the court in a grandly operatic way, 'I say to you that I will never repent the revolutionary course I have pursued for almost half a century. The only fight lost is the fight that has never taken place.'[57] There is no avoiding the fact that Tsigaridas possessed an outstanding talent and mind and had through his qualities as an outstanding thinker and organizer a deep impact on ELA's ideological, political and military strategy.

The constant factor in ELA's strategic history has been the absolute commitment to revolutionary objectives. These affected how ELA's leadership interpreted methods of resistance and guided the assumptions they made about their chosen strategies. ELA's overall persistence on the particular strategy of non-lethal low-level bombings, with the exception of the 1992–96 period, suggests that the domination of ideological symbolism over military activity and the employment of armed force was one significant factor that separated ELA from 17N. In the evolution of the two groups, both 17N and ELA aspired to be the ideological shapers and consciousness-raisers of the Greek working class, but 17N's revolutionary adventurism, militant nationalism, hunger for publicity and penchant for high-profile assassinations made it impossible for the two groups to establish an operational relationship and create a joint revolutionary front. As Tsigaridas put it: 'they may have both been organizations of the revolutionary left but there was an abyss of ideological, political and organizational differences between the two groups'.[58] Whereas 17N never disguised the centrality of violence to its strategy and organizational system, ELA's conception of the political environment was primarily one of social protest and resistance.

Revolutionary leaders often justify their actions by reference to the gains of future generations and Tsigaridas was no exception.[59] Reflecting on ELA's 20-year trajectory, Tsigaridas accepted that ELA had 'closed its historical circle'.[60] At the same time, however, he said that although 'evaluation of ELA's campaign was the job of the revolutionary movement to assess, one of ELA's main aims had been fulfilled; namely, that social reality in Greece is such that there will never be a shortage of armed revolutionary groups or revolutionary political action in the future'.[61] Tsigaridas' confidence in the actuality of a lasting revolutionary front was derived from the fact that through his five decades of political development, communist fighters like him had remained true to their principles and beliefs in the face of all pressures, setbacks and temptations. For those revolutionaries who over the years lost their faith and exited the movement, giving up on the revolution, Tsigaridas said that although renunciation and capitulation were never his thing, he took no issue with the fighters 'who moved away but kept a politically honourable and dignified stand'.[62] Tsiagaridas's perspective, however, was clear: the militant in revolutionary terms is a subject who must work hard, make sacrifices and, if necessary, die for the greater good. 'The passport of a revolutionary', he said, 'has no expiry date. It gets renewed every day and the stamps on it indicate the revolutionary's own actions. Because you were issued one to begin with, it does not mean that it will last you all your life. You need to have renewed it on a daily basis.'[63]

Prescribing violence, revolutionary or otherwise, as a historically justified response to political oppression, economic exploitation and imperialist aggression, the ELA theoretician urged the court not to 'deceive themselves'.[64] For 'political violence', Tsigaridas argued:

> characterizes exploitative societies for hundreds of years. It was not an ELA invention. And as long as there is exploitation and suppression, and as long as there is a will for getting rid of capitalist barbarity, and as long as people continue to live under occupation, revolutionary violence will be present.[65]

To illustrate his point, Tsigaridas used the Anglo-American invasion of Iraq and the Palestinian conflict to argue that the USA and Israel were much bigger killers of innocent people than their 'terrorist' foes.

For Tsigaridas, as one would expect from a communist guerrilla of undiminished ideological convictions, the class struggle continues to be permanent and fundamental and revolution was, is and remains the only road to take. 'I define myself as a revolutionary communist', he said to the court:

> And I refuse to give up my political work because at this given time nothing points towards a better future and because the crucial question of our age remains: communism or barbarism? As long as I remain free and to the degree that my health and my age allow me, I will be doing the work. I for one, together with many others of my generation, have made choices that defined our lives entirely. And for that I have no regrets.[66]

6

GREECE'S NEW GENERATION OF TERRORISTS

THE REVOLUTIONARY STRUGGLE (RS)

From its debut bomb attack on Athens' Evelpidon courthouse in September 2003, the Revolutionary Struggle (RS) terrorist group, *Epanastatikos Agonas* in Greek, seemed determined to make a bloody splash. Two bombs, timed to explode fifteen minutes apart with no advance notice, were designed to kill police responding to the first explosion at the courthouse. In the event, only one policeman was wounded. The RS attack was timed to coincide with the trial, held in Korydallos maximum-security prison, of Greece's premier (at the time) left-wing urban terrorist group, Revolutionary Organization 17 November (17N). In their second bombing at a Citibank branch in Neo Psychico, a northern Athens suburb, on 14 March 2004, RS placed a call thirty-five minutes before the time of the explosion, giving police barely enough time to disarm it with two controlled explosions. The next attack, on 5 May 2004, on a police station in the working class suburb of Kallithea, was a triple bomb attack and came just three months before the opening of the Athens Olympic Games. The first two bombs exploded within minutes of each other and the third about thirty minutes later, leading police to the conclusion that group intended to cause human casualties. The attack, somewhat inevitably, received huge press coverage prompting security experts and the international media to openly question Greece's resolve to provide ample safety and security measures for the first post-9/11 Games.

The RS Manifesto

Ten days after the Kallithea attack, RS issued a sixteen-page-long ideological manifesto-communiqué claiming responsibility for the triple bombing and publicizing the group's 'revolutionary' credentials. Entitled 'New World Order or the Terrorism International', a pun on the Communist International, the text outlined RS's political positions and purposes, offering at the same time a commentary on domestic and international conditions.[1] Like 17N, RS recognized that a clear, well-defined strategy and 'proper' justification of its actions would serve as an indicator of political effectiveness and ideological cohesion. RS, like 17N before them, offered an analysis of a society that required violence in order to be changed. Undertaking certain modes of action to affect its host political environment was deemed necessary by RS writers if Greece was to be liberated from a political system that it believed placed constitutional representative structures over popular interests. The group, in fact, saw its violence as a historically necessary and inevitable consequence of long-standing domestic sociopolitical conditions.

A mixture of ultra-leftist political analysis, international relations commentary and polemical hyperbole, 'New World Order or the Terrorism International' was very similar in style to past 17N communiqués and explored a number of themes ('the Greek political establishment', 'the trial of 17N' 'capitalist exploitation', 'globalization', '9/11', 'the US-led war on terror', 'the wars in Iraq and Afghanistan', 'the Arab-Israeli conflict' and the 'US hegemonic plans in the Balkans', to name a few) from which the group drew inspiration and motivation for its campaign. In an attempt to display intellectual depth, broaden their political appeal and thus increase the group's respectability and prestige vis-à-vis their audience, RS writers presented their case in a jargon-ridden style which blended Marxist scientific pretence with trenchant obloquy that did not necessarily strengthen nor advance their general argument.

The group devoted the opening section of 'New World Order or the Terrorism International' to explaining why it had to take up arms and why commitment to the idea of revolution had become its central tenet. In surveying contemporary world politics in the first decade of the new century, RS argued that the current conflict clearly evinced a battle between the forces of revolution and counter-revolution. The twenty-first century, the group declared:

> will belong to those peoples, communities and political groups who will not surrender without a fight against modern totalitarianism, who will not submit to the terrorism of the new war, who will resist the plans of the dominators for subjugation of the peoples, for repression of the struggles, for conquest of the world. It will belong to those who will not choose to remain silent, to those who will choose to resist and struggle for freedom. A new world societal and class conflict is underway...[2]

Searching, at the same time, for a way to insert itself into Greek political discourse, RS used its manifesto to gain sympathy and galvanize left-wing extremists into action. The text was deliberately designed to identify the group with concerns of the Greek masses and to capitalize on public perceptions. As such, RS writers went for 17N's tried-and-tested formula of putting the blame for Greece's current predicament on the country's political and financial elite. RS's critical barrage was particularly directed against the former Socialist prime minister Costas Simitis who in 1996 took over from Andreas Papandreou and went on to serve a record eight consecutive years.

Determined to expose what it saw as obvious but unspoken social and political truths, RS said that looking back on the administrative and bureaucratic state structures that shaped the past decade was to survey a scene of wreckage. Sarcastically referring to Simitis as 'the socialist-liberal modernizer', the group argued that the strategy of modernization his socialist governments sought to carry through—aimed supposedly at a major transformation of the economy and society—proved not only completely inadequate to the nature and scope of the problem, but also involved a vicious attack on its own social base. The core argument was that Simitis's technocratic economic management combined with slavishly followed neoliberal free-market practices caused extensive damage to the fabric of Greek society. In a paragraph of sustained invective, RS writers scorned Simitis for investing a great deal of rhetorical energy in his 'powerful Greece' narrative, concluding that 'this so-called powerful Greece' was built at the expense of the majority of 'long suffering low-paid workers', who were 'the majority and live on the poverty line'.[3]

In Simitis' fantastical creation of 'powerful and modern Greece', the group trenchantly declared, the majority:

> live under the daily terrorism of poverty, unemployment and over-indebtedness to the banking vampires. It is a majority that is not entitled to go on strike, given that in the otherwise 'free and democratic' environment

> industrial actions are criminalized and prosecuted...This powerful and modern Greece is the Greece of the MAT [the riot police] which attacks protesters in demonstrations. This powerful Greece is being built with the blood of dead workers who, between 1999 and to date exceed 750, in a total of work-related accidents reaching 20,000. This powerful Greece is being fed by the bleeding the immigrants who are forced to live in modern-day slave trade conditions...[4]

This was the reality, RS declared, and warned that 'this reality was to be perpetuated and legitimized every four years through elections'.[5] RS also said that it was under no illusion that what lay ahead was 'even greater poverty, even greater unemployment, even more social exclusion'.[6] As RS further explained, there were two choices: 'either strengthen the existing barbarity through our inactivity, or through action cancel the system's "omnipotence", rupture acquiescence, and dissipate social fear which today is the basic component of modern hegemony'.[7] Declaring its determination to keep the momentum of armed violence, RS urged its readers to reject 'this rotten regime' and line themselves up against 'its apologists whichever political area they may come from'.[8]

RS Targets Greek Cabinet Minister

In May 2006, the group targeted for the first time a Greek politician, the then Culture Minister George Voulgarakis. A remote-controlled bomb with 2.5 kilos of dynamite, exploded just 200 meters from Voulgarakis' apartment, at the foot of Lycabettus Hill in central Athens, causing a great deal of material damage but no injuries. Voulgarakis, who had been Public Order Minister until February of that year, was targeted, RS said, in an eleven-page proclamation, because, during his term as public order minister, he used the 2004 Athens Olympic Games, as a pretext for introducing 'Orwellian' counter-terrorism legislation and presiding over a massive security upgrade of the Greek state. It was primarily thanks to the efforts of politicians like him, the group said, that 'we have now entered the age of the Terrorism of Mass Surveillances'. Explaining this was not difficult, the group added:

> During his time as Public Order Minister and with the Olympic Games as pretext—which in many ways benefited the Greek financial and political elite—he introduced new provisions which enriched the counter-terrorism legislation, while for the first time Greece implemented such a

> large-scale new "defence dogma" of a single area for military and police surveillance. NATO and the secret services of several countries had a free rein in our country before and during the Olympic Games, invited by the government and tolerated by the opposition. The security measures for the Games even included mass telephone tapping of citizens and Voulgarakis himself undertook to convince the multinational telecommunications companies to cooperate with the state in order to implement this. The continuation, or rather the increase, of tapping even after the Olympics by both the Greek and foreign secret services, which is being called a scandal, not merely because it gave an unprecedented dimension to the policing of all our lives but also because it was done by sidestepping existing institutions, principles and laws.[9]

The 'second reason' why Voulgarakis was targeted by RS was his role in the alleged abduction and torture of twenty-eight Pakistani immigrants by Greek intelligence agents a week after the London bombings of 7 July 2005. The reason the twenty-eight were targeted was apparently because their phone numbers appeared in an electronic trail that British detectives were keen to pursue. As Voulgarakis told MPs in a subsequent parliamentary inquiry after the case of the Pakistanis became a cause celebre in Greece when a public prosecutor began a formal investigation, the British authorities soon after 7/7 asked the Greeks to investigate suspicious phone calls made by people they suspected of being al-Qaeda sympathisers. An under-pressure Voulgarakis also revealed that over the course of two months, 5,000 economic migrants were questioned by Greek security although he insisted rather unconvincingly that the twenty-eight Pakistanis were not among the 5,000 rounded up. The group said that the implications of the incident went deeper than it appeared at first sight. In RS's view, the abduction of the Pakistani immigrants was not simply a case of the violation of individual rights, it was much more than that. It constituted 'a hostile act against Muslims which could lead to Islamist reprisals against Greece'.[10] To make the point clearer still, the group said that 'the attacks in London and Madrid showed that the victims of such reprisals were ultimately not the state officials themselves, like Karamanlis [the Greek PM] and Voulgarakis in this specific case, who took the criminal decisions, but the ordinary people who suffer the consequences from the criminal politicians'. The final step in RS's argument was that the divergence in counter-terrorism measures and their subsequent abuses of law and human rights underlined the need to develop what the group called 'a substantive international solidarity with all those who are being hurt by the New World financial and political order'. The group did not go so far as to suggest the launching of a European guerrilla war but it did make the point that armed revolutionary actions 'against the member countries of the neo-imperialist alliance' could have a double effect: they could be seen as 'a dynamic political response' and also function as a deterrent against the hostile retribution by armed Islamists.[11] The communiqué ended, however, with a threat to the Greek establishment: 'although we failed this time, this does not mean that we will fail the next time we choose to attack a lowlife of the political or economic authority'.[12]

Attacking the 'US Terrorists'

RS's determination to attack the mechanisms which supported the US-imposed New World Order's economic and political structures culminated in the early-morning January 2007 attack against the US embassy in Athens. This was not the first time that the US embassy, one of the most fortified and tightly guarded buildings in the region, came under attack by left-wing guerrillas. In 1996, 17N marked its twenty years of violence with an IRA-style mortar attack against the embassy. Modelling its attack on the 1996 one, the RS grenade was launched from a hand-held Soviet designed rocket-propelled RGP-7 at 5:58 a.m., apparently from across the six lanes of Vassilisis Sophia Boulevard, opposite the embassy, the main north-south road in central Athens in the densely populated Ilissia neighbourhood. The RS commandos aimed at the US embassy emblem on the front of the building. However, the projectile narrowly missed its intended target, damaging instead a bathroom on the third floor, which housed the ambassador's office, and shattering windows in nearby buildings. The use of the RGP-7 denoted the group's determination to raise the level of its tactical sophistication and affirmed its ambition to follow in the operational footsteps of 17N.

The six-page communiqué sent to the media a fortnight after the attack did not hide the authors' ideological viewpoint on American power and influence on events and international developments. Surveying the current state of Greek-US relations, RS lamented that Greece's political and economic dependence on the superpower was on the increase rather than on the decline. Like 17N before them, RS writers argued that the continuing impact of US presence on Greek soil humiliated the Greek people and disfigured all aspects of life in the country. RS deplored the fact that the United States continued 'and will continue to be the big boss of the Greek governments' which, from the end of the Cold War onwards had totally aligned themselves with each and every US policy on all the burning issues concerning the wider region, from the Balkans and Cyprus to the Middle East.[13]

Conveying its rage through the dramatized style of the text, RS declared that the slogan, 'Americans, Murderers of the People', so often heard for so many decades in Greece, was an accurate reflection of the present-day nature of US foreign policy[14]. 'If we could imagine', the group said, 'a generalized popular uprising taking place in Greece, which we wish for and are striving for with all our might, it is more than certain that the first building to be demolished would be the US embassy.'[15] RS's essential point was that their attack against the embassy could provide a critical impetus sending a message that 'in Greece there will be resistance and there will be armed struggle against the New World Order'. Underpinning the entire communiqué was a conviction that a sustained campaign of armed resistance against dispossession, US terrorism and global hegemony would disrupt American imperialism's war plans:

> How else could the Iraqi people have caused such a serious problem for the superpower and its allies had they not chosen armed resistance? ... Would they have achieved anything with peaceful marches and protestations, with referendums and participation in the occupation governments? No, they wouldn't. How else could Hezbollah have effectively resisted the Israeli invasion without its weapons and infrastructure?...Both cases show that armed actions and rebellion by determined social and political forces are capable of creating serious problems for military forces possessing arms superiority, of unsettling the superpower politically, of creating cracks in the 'counter-terrorist' alliance and of checking the charge of the New World Order.[16]

The communiqué ended both with a dedication and a hope. The group dedicated its attack on the embassy to 'the Iraqi resistance crushing the US war machine, the Hezbollah in Lebanon and to the armed Palestinian organizations battling Israeli occupation'.[17] At the same time, the group remained hopeful that rising social unrest would herald new conflict and new forms of dynamic political action, further exposing the regime's vulnerability. From this point on, the group's ambition to maintain a politically effective voice on national issues would be inseparable from its determination to expel the American bases and NATO forces Greek soil, 'overthrowing, in the process, the criminal, political and economic system that collaborates with them'.[18]

Responding to Bullets with Bullets

The next 'traditional' target to come under attack was the Greek police. Between April 2007 and January 2009, the group carried out three separate attacks against a police station, a MAT riot police bus and a three-member strong police unit on foot patrol, leaving a twenty-one-year old member of the unit in critical condition. The police patrol came under fire at the rear of the Culture Ministry building in Exarchia, nearly exactly a month after the killing of fifteen-year-old Alexis Grigoropoulos by a police officer on 6 December 2009, which led to two weeks of rioting with gangs of youths smashing, looting and burning shops across the country in protest at heavy-handed police tactics. The last time a policeman killed a teenager was in November 1985, when fifteen-year old Michalis Kaltezas was shot dead by a stray police bullet during a march to the American embassy to mark the anniversary of the November 1973 Polytechnic student revolt. 17N's response, at the time, to the Kaltezas incident was almost immediate. A week after the incident, the group detonated a remote-controlled car bomb against a MAT riot police bus, fatally injuring one and wounding another fourteen. 17N justified the attack by arguing that police brutality was an indicator of Greek contemporary society and explained that the violence of the regime had to be met not with an ideological fight but with popular militant violence.[19]

RS saw the Grigoropoulos incident in the same way 17N saw the Kaltezas one two and a half decades earlier: an opportunity to generate armed struggle propaganda and gain public sympathy. By using violence 'in the name of the people' in order to respond, punish and retaliate against state violence, RS hoped to establish a dialogue with the community and justify its existence as the military extension of the movement. In an eleven-page communiqué, entitled 'We Respond to Bullets with Bullets', the group explained that the attack against the police patrol was a response to the 'cowardly murder' of Grigoropoulos. RS said that 6 December, when Grigoropoulos died, signalled the end of:

> a staggering social normality which the state was at pains to impose, within an atmosphere of deep social crisis, with the prime means being policing

> and repression. The social outrage boiled over and the violent uprising that followed dissipated whatever self-delusions there were that the existing regime of representative democracy is based on society's consent. And it has now been understood by everyone that the dividing line between the fellow travelers of the regime and those who fight it has taken such dimensions which highlight an irreversible social and political rupture and give forewarning of the coming generalized social collision.[20]

RS saw the application of armed response as the most effective form of defence against the regime's 'ruthless uniformed thugs' who have 'declared war on anyone who in any way turns against them'.[21] Against this, the group issued a warning to all those in the movement 'who believed that the situation could be reversed through peaceful demonstrations and protests'. Those who entertain such illusions, the group said, 'together with those who seriously think that the cop's mentality will change, are those who will end up as the next victims of state terrorism'.[22]

At the same time, the group made no bones about its ambition to serve as the as the *primum mobile* of the Greek revolutionary movement. In combative tone, the group declared that their attack, apart from avenging Grigoropoulos's death, was intended to show 'not only the necessity for but also the effectiveness of armed action'.[23] In RS's conception, an armed confrontation with the regime was not only desirable but achievable. It was true, it added, that 'we may not have the training or the arsenal the cops have, but we are determined and armed primarily with our faith. What we showed is that if a few fighters managed in the most policed area of Athens to come face-to-face with the regime's guards and to humiliate them operationally, then we can imagine what could be achieved by a mass armed revolutionary movement'.[24]

At the same time, RS took issue with sections of the extra-parliamentary left that had been critical of the group's methods. Commenting on the fact that various anti-authoritarian organizations had accused the group of damaging the movement with its actions, RS asserted that this was a ready-made argument which was all too often served as an excuse for not carrying out any meaningful discussion about the necessity of violence and its organised practice. Advocating that 'social uprising and revolutions cannot but be everywhere and be violent', RS attacked the extra-parliamentary left as 'the movement's KKE' whose legalism, pacifism and daily compromises meant that like the real KKE, the Greek Communist Party, would never come close to bringing about meaningful revolutionary change. Despite paying lip-service to the contrary, the group asserted, these 'sweet water revolutionaries' have done absolutely nothing to regain a sense of the revolutionary goal apart from 'issuing newspapers and brochures and staging events and peaceful demonstrations'. This drove the RS to the conclusion that 'these people were only interested in their "political shop" and not in the revolutionary movement and the revolution'.[25]

At the same time, RS argued that radicalizing the masses through the transformation of their attitudes towards existing authority relationships was and would remain the group's overriding priority. To further this point the group said that the December events had provided a new, powerful political momentum. Convinced that Greek society was 'a boiling pot', and that the 'atmosphere taking shape was explosive', the group declared confidently that 'for the first time in many decades a way was opening for destabilization from the bottom of the regime'.[26] Posing as representative of the entire community, the group even suggested that 'a discussion should immediately begin between all the revolutionary forces about the prospect of a liberated social, political and economic organization, through a series of revolutionary priorities regarding work, promotion, daily life.'[27]

RS Adopts Car Bombing

Despite police pressure, the tempo of RS attacks in 2009 increased and operations became more spectacular. After a failed attempt to detonate a booby-trapped car with 150 kilos of ammonium-nitrate-fuel-oil (ANFO) against Citibank's headquarters in Kifissia in February of that year, RS's determination to sustain a high level of anxiety among Greece's business establishment culminated, seven months later, in the detonation of a powerful car bomb outside the Athens Stock Exchange. The bomb was hidden in a stolen van parked behind the new modernist building on Athinon Avenue in the city's western suburbs. The blast caused extensive damage to the building, blowing out windows and spreading chunks of concrete and shards of glass hundreds of metres away. It also caused minor injuries to a female cleaner who had been at work in a nearby apartment building.[28]

The attack on the Athens Stock Exchange (ASE) was intended to highlight the severity of Greece's accumulated economic problems arising from a conflict of interests between 'dominant group of plutocrats and exploited classes' within society. In a twenty-seven-page-long text which read more like an academic paper than a communiqué, the group made an attempt to develop and give substance to the view that the deep polarizations, running from top to bottom of Greece's inequality-riven society, were the product of systemic institutional and economic causes. Lamenting the fact that the explosion, despite the substantial damage it caused to the building, failed to stop trading, RS went on to explain why the Greek stock exchange, indissolubly linked with the history of the country's existing economic system, constituted one of the most powerful and effective levers for drawing wealth from the base of society and transferring it to the minority economic elite. RS writers wanted to leave the reader in little doubt that the ASE was 'a mechanism that loots, and sucks out the juice from the productive social product without offering anything at all in return'. Referring contemptuously to the ASE as 'a paradise for profiteering for supranational capital', it added that the profits of the stock exchange 'bubbles' were filling the pockets of Greek capitalists and their fellow foreign players while the majority of Greek society was drowning in the storm of the global economic crisis.[29] The group insisted that modern capitalism had arrived at a moral death but it was important to understand the reasons why and how societies across the globe had been 'hoodwinked by a collection of greedy, deceitful chancers, in the guise of investment bankers, hedge and private equity fund partners and bankers who had taken the world to what will be the longest lasting financial crisis in the history of the capitalist system'.[30] RS believed that by attacking the ASE it attacked 'greed, deceit, self-enrichment, scandalous privileges of tax exemptions, capitalist exploitation and corporate kleptocracy' which were the root causes for the country's economic decline, total stagnation and miserable working class living standards.

With the general election only weeks away (4 October 2009), the group also used the bombing as an occasion to reaffirm its determination to 'participate' in the political process. Mocking the leadership of the two main political parties (PA.SO.K. and New Democracy) for having 'identical strategies' in dealing with the economic crisis, 'namely to protect capital and profits while the plundering raid and neoliberal attack against the vulnerable sections of Greek society not only goes on but intensifies', RS asked Greek voters to 'turn their back on the political system' and abstain from the forthcoming elections.[31] The group used the historically unprecedented high abstention rate of 48 per cent in the June 2009 European elections to argue that 'it was becoming obvious to more and more people that the regime and its institutions are rotten and that no political party inspires confidence and hope for a better tomorrow'.[32] At the same time, the group was under no illusion that 'those who did not vote last time are now one step short of the revolutionary charge' but abstention none the less could be 'the starting point for an honest unsullied struggle for social emancipation'.[33]

The Death of Lambros Foundas

In the early hours of the morning on 11 March 2010, in the southeastern Athens neighbourhood of Dafni, two men inside a Seat Ibiza are approached by a police car. As soon as the officers turn their headlights on, the two passengers jump out of the car and start firing. During the exchange, thity-five-year-old Lambros Foundas is shot dead, while his accomplice manages to escape. Next to the body of the fatally wounded Foundas (who wore double leather gloves and had no phone or ID), lies a Zastava handgun, with two bullets missing from the chamber, a walkie-talkie and backpack with a handmade bomb of a similar type used in previous RS operations. The stolen Seat Ibiza was, police believed, to be used in an operation within the next twenty-four hours.

A known political activist, Foundas, as a high school student, joined the anarchist group Mavro Agathi (Black Thorn) that issued the 'Dromi tis Orgis' (Streets of Rage) pamphlet and participated in marches, rallies and school occupations, particularly after the murder of leftist school teacher Nikos Temponeras in 1991 in the Greek city of Patras by the then secretary of the youth branch of the New Democracy right-wing party. The killing caused civil unrest in several Greek towns for days, especially in Athens, where four protesters died, and in Patras, where the Town Hall and the city's police station were burned down following a 25,000 strong demonstration. The civil unrest stopped only after the Minister of Education resigned. Foundas, a microbiologist, had been known to the police since November 1995 when he was arrested together with another 500 militants during the occupation of the Athens Polytechnic to mark the anniversary of the 1973 uprising.

A police examination of the contents of Foundas's mobile phone and laptop provided the authorities with a list of suspects which led to the surveillance and arrests, after raids on several properties in Athens, of five men and one woman, aged between thirty and forty-one who were subsequently charged with multiple counts of attempted homicide, causing explosions and armed offences linked with RS. Police announced that during a search of the home of Nikos Maziotis, aged thirty-nine—believed by the police to be the group's leader of operations—they found original RS communiqués, hand-drawn plans of future targets and detailed road maps for upcoming strikes.

In 1999, Maziotis was convicted and given a three-and-a-half year prison sentence for planting a bomb, which failed to explode, outside the Ministry of Development building in December 1997 in protest against the installation of a gold metallurgy by multinational company TVX Gold in the village of Strymonikos, Halkidiki in northern Greece. Throughout the trial Maziotis refused to accept the charges and defended his choices ideologically, insisting on having nothing to apologize for because he did not consider himself 'a criminal'. 'I am a revolutionary', he told the court, 'and for that I have nothing to repent. The only I regret I have is the technical error that was made and that the bomb failed to explode, so my fingerprint was found on it and I ended up here. This is the only thing I repent.'[34] Commitment to ideology as a guide for political action pervaded Maziotis' court testimony. Advocating 'social revolution by any means necessary', he argued that it was generally 'proven in Greek but also in international social and political history that no changes ever came about, and never did humanity achieve any progress—progress as I see it—through begging, through praying or by words alone'.[35] With absolute conviction of rightness, Maziotis said that placing the bomb was not 'an act of terrorism but an act of solidarity. Revolutionaries and the militants' were not the terrorists. The actual terrorists were 'the states themselves'.[36]

The End of RS?

The shackles of post-17N 'revolutionary' expectation were a burden that RS attempted to break from early on. In a certain sector of Greek public consciousness, 17N will always be positioned at the intersection between 'popular avengers' and 'armed revolutionaries'. Believing that 17N's revolutionary experiment could only be surpassed by a new revolutionary experiment, RS's overriding objective was to 'shape a genuine revolutionary current, equal to the requirements of the age'.[37] In that sense, RS embraced 17N's view of terrorist violence as a legitimate and logical form of expression for those humiliated and ridiculed by the ruthless capitalist mechanisms of power.

RS's central ambition was, to use the words of a senior Greek counter-terrorism officer, to 'stand alongside 17N in the Greek pantheon of great revolutionary forces' even though the group out of 'revolutionary modesty' would never admit it.[38] RS, like all organizations which resort to terrorism, claimed that its cause justified extremism. The group presented themselves and their violence in terms of political dissent, moral conviction and armed insurrection. Narrating its discourse through lengthy attack communiqués which, thanks to 17N, have long become an established Greek media ritual, RS elaborated the presentation of political events and expanded the dimensions of their violent context in an attempt to dramatize the anomalies of the existing system, deny its legitimacy and propound alternative models. The group believed that it was a priority to create an insurrectionary mood which would awaken consciences and radicalize people. Utterly convinced that the 'age offers unique opportunities for anyone wishing to fight', RS sought to take the role of vanguard of the movement and persuade other groups making up the panorama of Greek extra-parliamentary left that 'conditions for an overthrow of the system by revolutionary armed struggle are ripe'.[39] In fact, as far as the group was concerned 'the conditions were never better'.[40] RS held it as axiomatic that 'the regime had entered a phase of destabilization and would therefore be 'exceedingly vulnerable' if attacked with increasing violence. As such, the group's modus operandi incorporated high-profile assassination attempts, armed raids, car bombings and rocket attacks in order to promote a generalized sense of terror.

In the long run all terrorist groups eventually end, even in Greece. But the longer it takes, the more people die and the more damage is caused. It is worth remembering that for an astonishing twenty-seven years, from the mid-1970s up to 2002, 17N pursued one of the most intransigent campaigns of terrorism in Europe, assassinating US and British diplomats, Greek politicians, newspaper publishers and industrialists, detonating hundreds of bombs and firing rockets against foreign embassies and businesses, causing hundreds of millions of euros of damage to property. It is also worth remembering that in all this time successive Greek governments failed to bring to justice even one member of the group and, in the end, it was a only a massive blunder on the part of the terrorists that led to their arrests and the group's demise. History may well judge 17N as a failure, but this does not alter the fact that they succeeded in running rings round the Greek authorities primarily because they took advantage of the fact that Greece's national counter-terrorism effort was conducted for more than two decades against a background of half-measures, polarization, rivalry and exaggeration. Greece's state response to 17N violence can in fact be used as an excellent case-study of what *not* to do when dealing with terrorism.

History began to repeat itself when RS emerged, for Greece's state response to RS amounted to nothing more substantial than the usual 'the terrorists are ruthless criminals' and 'the perpetrators will be brought to justice' empty government rhetoric. The truth is that the Greek state seemed to be following the same lethargic, dilatory, if not indifferent, anti-terrorism approach that had served the country so badly in the past. When a terrorist war begins, there has to be a reason for every bombing and each shooting. This is the one lesson that Greek authorities should have learned after the 17N fiasco, and they therefore should have taken the RS terrorist threat they faced far more seriously.

But, like 17N during the group's early years, RS seemed to be receiving the same weak anti-terrorism treatment. Rather than sending the terrorists an early and clear signal that violence would not be tolerated, the Greek state authorities seemed to be in denial, acting as if there was no problem. A considerable number of senior officials the author spoke with at the Ministry of Public Order at the time[41] were seriously entertaining the theory that 17N's dismantling had brought the final victory over terrorism in Greece, insisting that whatever small splinter groups still remained, they posed no real security threat. Unsurprisingly, this inability on the part of Greece's security community to assess accurately the real danger RS posed gave the terrorists enough time to organize and improve in operational terms. The group's leader, Maziotis, was apparently able to act with impunity despite being known to the police watch list since the late 1990s when he was put behind bars for placing the bomb that never detonated outside the Development Ministry. One would expect that upon his release in August 2001 such a person would be placed under close police surveillance. Obviously, he was not, because if he was being watched then one has to wonder how he managed to allegedly coordinate more than a dozen attacks, including bombings, rocket attacks and armed raids.[42]

However, the 2009 election of a new government changed all that. The return of Michalis Chrysohoidis, who was in charge during the 17N breakup, to the Ministry of Public Order and the inevitable change of all top police, counter-terrorism and national intelligence personnel for reasons of political patronage, however bad a reflection on Greece's political culture it was, meant that Chrysohoidis surrounded himself with people he trusted and whose specialized knowledge and experience was vital in rooting out 17N back in the summer of 2002. As one of his senior counter-terrorism officials put it: 'Maziotis and his "friends" were extremely dangerous and violent people and they would murder a lot of people if allowed to continue. The lessons of the recent past were considered, comprehended and carefully calibrated for the particular circumstances and the particular strategy of the group in question.'[43]

The RS could still regroup and make a comeback but with six of its core members captured in April 2010 the group, with Maziotis and his partner and comrade Panagiota Roupa behind bars, would face an uphill battle to maintain momentum. According to sources close to the Public Order Minister, the group could only count on around another three, maximum four members still at liberty, leaving the organization to face a profound period of crisis that could, and probably will, become definitive.[44] It would be a mistake to think, however, that the logistical and operational dismantling of RS marked the end of revolutionary terrorism in Greece. As will be seen in the next chapter, other post-17N groups such as the Conspiracy of the Cells Fire (CCF) took the baton of violence from RS, which is why it remains of critical importance that Greece's security forces finally relied less on luck to stop terrorists in the future and more on a coherent anti-terror strategy and an integrated counter-terrorism capability. As the graffiti that appeared, only days after the arrests of Maziotis and his fellow RS members, on numerous walls in central Athens has it: 'Nothing is finished, it all continues'.

Timeline of RS attacks

5 September 2003	Double bombing at Evelpidon courthouse; one policeman injured
14 March 2004	Police defuse bomb at Citibank in Neo Psychiko
5 May 2004	Three bombs set at Kallithea police precinct, three months before Athens Olympics

29 October 2004	Bomb placed near MAT riot police bus
2 June 2005	Bomb explodes outside Labour Ministry
12 December 2005	Three injured by bomb outside Finance Ministry
30 May 2006	Bomb explodes near home of former public order minister George Voulgarakis
12 January 2007	Rocket-propelled grenade crashes through window at the US embassy in Athens
30 April 2007	Shooting at Nea Ionia precinct and handgrenade thrown
24 October 2008	Bomb defused by police at Shell Oil office in Faliro
23 December 2008	Gunfire from a Kalashnikov assault rifle directed at MAT riot police bus near Polytechnic campus
5 January 2009	Policeman seriously injured by Kalashnikov gunfire near Culture Ministry
18 February 2009	Unexploded car bomb found at Citibank headquarters
9 March 2009	Bomb placed near Citibank in Filothei
12 May 2009	Bomb explodes at Eurobank in Argyroupolis
2 September 2009	Car bomb explodes near Athens Stock Exchange

7

GREECE'S NEW GENERATION OF TERRORISTS, PART 2

THE CONSPIRACY OF CELLS OF FIRE (CCF)

On Monday 21 January 2008, just after midnight, a previously unknown group set off a barrage of firebomb attacks against widely dispersed bank branches, luxury car dealerships and Public Power Company vehicles in Athens and Salonica, all within a thirty-minute period. A previously unknown group called the Conspiracy of Cells of Fire (CCF) took responsibility for the attacks the next day in a document sent to an Athenian website. The declared purpose of the attacks was to express solidarity with the imprisoned anarchist Vangelis Botzatzis and three other fugitive comrades, all involved in numerous arson attacks against banks. The number and coordination of CCF attacks—multiple four-person teams on motorbikes—alarmed the Greek police, but investigators were preoccupied with the more lethal and more dangerous Revolutionary Struggle (RS) group operating at the same time. The next CCF barrage of fire bombings came a month later with the group detonating incendiary devices on eight separate targets across parts of Athens. In its initial phase of activity, CCF averaged one arson wave a month, in both Athens and Salonica, often simultaneously. Early attacks[1] focused on symbols rather than human beings as the group seemed reluctant to escalate its military methods and strategy.

CCF's attack communiqués, written by different writers in markedly different literary styles, were brief and to the point, seeking to create a feeling of revolt and resistance against modern power structures, lack of representation and the hierarchies of capitalist society. Solidarity with local and foreign anarchists and visceral hatred of banks, 'the military-police complex', consumer society and the political establishment were among the central themes of CCF's communiqués during its first year. CCF employed a strategy of arson because, as it explained in its first communiqué, 'the revolutionary element of arson against economic-capitalist targets is not only in its material destruction but also in the choice of the attack and the transgressiveness of the act'.[2] Viewing itself as 'anarcho-revolutionary', CCF embraced revolutionary guerrilla warfare but did not attempt, like its contemporary RS, to fit itself into Greek left-wing political traditions by formulating class-based criticisms of the Greek state. CCF justified its campaign of terrorism with an ideology that largely resembled radical anarcho-communist traditions. 'Striking at the ordinary flow of the system', CCF's violence was intended to compensate the coercive character of capitalism and modern mechanisms of domination. The group's search for a way to insert itself into Greek political discourse meant that both attacks and attack communiqués took on a progressively violent character. After a three day arson spree against several bank branches, a police bus, city hall offices and offices and vehicles of private security firms, CCF said its terrorism was 'becoming part of a generalized attack against the present state, a defence of our freedom, a part of the destruction of your world'.[3]

The December 2008 Events and the Greek Anti-Authority Movement

On 6 December 2008, the fatal shooting of a fifteen-year-old student, near Exarchia Square in central Athens by a policeman, unleashed the worst civil violence in decades that spread like wildfire all over the country, lasting for more than a week. The death of Alexis Grigoropoulos[4] resulted in large protests and demonstrations that escalated to widespread rioting, looting, street violence and ultimately small-scale terrorism. The last time a Greek policeman had killed a schoolboy was in November 1985, when fifteen-year-old Michalis Kaltezas was shot dead by a stray police bullet during a march to the American embassy to mark the anniversary of the November 1973 Polytechnic student revolt. The Kaltezas incident unleashed another wave of protests, riots and occupations that culminated a week after the incident in 17N, the premier terrorist group at the time, detonating a remote-controlled car bomb against a Greek MAT riot police bus, fatally injuring one and wounding another fourteen.

The December events had a direct and profound influence on the post-17N terrorist scene as it overwhelmed the anarchist/anti-authority movement with newly emerged groups. In their desire to establish their credibility, these new groups engaged in violent rhetoric and increasingly aggressive forms of action. For more established groups such as CCF, this new mood of militancy reinforced the group's resolve and intensified its revolutionary ambitions. Determined to broaden its aims and expand its influence, CCF pledged to wage a 'new, rabid armed struggle'. As a result, the period between mid-December 2008 and February 2009 was packed with incident, with CCF raiding a police college with Molotov cocktails and carrying out over thirty arson bomb attacks.

CCF's subsequent attack communiqué was dedicated to the jailed 17N chief of operations, Dimitris Koufodinas, 'urban guerrilla and one of the very few authentic revolutionaries who never gave in and never capitulated'.[5] The untitled communiqué read like a manifesto as it sought to link armed violence, class war and the revolutionary process. The text, polemical yet less flamboyant than previous communiqués, did not present—as one would have expected—the group's full take on the post-December 2008 landscape. CCF concentrated instead on past 'struggles and sacrifices' of urban guerrilla, reflecting, at the same time, on the political possibilities open to the revolutionary movement. Over the last few months, CCF said, urban guerrilla struggle:

> has become one of the most popular topics for discussion in intellectual circles, among historians and progressive leftists. Books, movies, documentaries, debates on TV alternately mention or admonish comrades "who made the wrong choice". The bottom line is that they have all reached the same conclusion, interpreting urban guerrilla struggle as a historical defeat and a political cul-de-sac. Their "mathematical" logic that explains revolutionary practices in terms of numbers of arrests, incinerations and deaths is totally divorced from any dialectical proposition. Following their logic, we then need to ask: have there been any forms of struggle that have not been defeated? Have there been any mass movements, mobilizations and protest activity that resulted in overturning what they fought against? The German RAF, the Italian Red Brigades, the French Action Directe, the Spanish MIL, the English Angry Brigade all constitute even today central themes of discussion among young comrades, proving that their military

> defeat did not cancel out lessons and experiences of past struggles and the entire revolutionary process.[6]

The main weight of the communiqué, however, fell on what urban armed struggle signified for CCF and how present-day groups like themselves compared with past ones. In surveying the recent history of armed campaigns, CCF paid tribute to them but granted at the same time, that the desire of those groups to link themselves to a broader level of social and ideological conflict, demonstrated in the choice of the targets and the forms of intervention, was invested with ambiguous political meanings. Armed organizations, CCF explained, 'always searched for a revolutionary subject' which subsequently defined the organization's agenda. 'For the Red Brigades, it was the workers in the car factories, for the 17N it was defending the Greek populace, for RAF it was the liberation of the Third World etc. For all of them, armed struggle constituted a process of acceleration for class war.'[7]

Primarily a commentary on the shape of things to come, the communiqué was directed at ideological friends and foes alike. Its fundamental point was to confirm CCF's determination to entrench their activity in a broader territorial context and supply a new basis for the political organizations that were willing to take a revolutionary direction. In the final section of the communiqué, CCF stressed its determination to foment revolution. The group paid tribute to 17N and ELA but was equally emphatic that these groups had fulfilled their historical function and an alternative organizational structure was needed. Willing to pursue a pattern of urban guerrilla warfare that differed from the one carried out before, CCF vowed to produce a new vocabulary to describe revolutionary political solidarities.

Democracy Shall Not Prevail

On 9 June 2010, CCF detonated a bomb outside the Greek parliament in central Athens. Police were able to clear the area around the building after receiving a fifteen-minute warning ahead of the blast. The blast blew out some of the parliament building's windows but no one was injured in the attack. CCF had placed the bomb in a rubbish bin close to the Tomb of the Unknown Soldier, in Syntagma Square in one of the busiest areas of the Greek capital. Given the fact that parliament was in session at the time of the attack, this was CCF's way of saying that they could strike against one of the most heavily guarded buildings in the country with impunity. A five-page communiqué entitled 'Democracy Shall Not Prevail', a reversal of the Greek premier's recent statement that 'democracy will prevail', was posted to athens.indymedia.org, a website where the group would send its texts after each operation.

Citing excerpts[8] from T.S Eliot's *The Hollow Men*, a poem about Guy Fawkes's attempt to blow up the British Parliament, CCF writers discussed both the failure of governability and the revolutionary potentiality in Greece. CCF's attack focused primarily on current parliamentary forms of democratic representation and the dysfunctional sociopolitical and economic structures of Greek society. Although CCF's criticism of Greek representative democracy did have a genuine edge to it, the text's often abrasive tone and obvious irritation on the writers' part gave the communiqué a fragmented quality of political analysis.

The first quarter of the communiqué was devoted to the dominant presuppositions of Greece's democratic culture. 'If it sounds unthinkable in our days', the group said:

> for anyone to speak against democracy without being labelled a right-wing conservative or a fascist, it is because propaganda resides in the houses and in the minds of democracy's own subjects. Democracy's totalitarianism has otherwise nothing to envy from previous totalitarian regimes. Nepotism, aristocracy, men of the court, businessmen, middlemen, contractors and publishers still rule social life, while the ones down below remain unjustly treated and at the same time, always willing to be fooled.[9]

The reason for that is not hard to find, CCF explained, given that:

> ordinary Greeks want to take their place which is why they continue to passively tolerate them. The ambitions of easy enrichment, spectacular social advancement, a professional career, assets and material acquisition are what democratic prosperity has come to promise. And so, the wilful subjects surrender to the totalitarianism of capitalist domination against a democratic background. The exploitation of our labour and of our lives intensifies, social disparities widen, the world's police forces become militarised, and intellectual and emotional wretchedness becomes the only choice of the many.[10]

Not that any of this was new, CCF said, far from it. 'This, more or less, has been the stage set for social life under the yoke of any authority. Today, however, democracy sugar-coats the bitter pill.'[11] The point was, CCF said, that liberal democracy had now reverted into 'a coup d'état that doesn't actually send tanks out on the streets [a reference to the

Greek Colonels' 1967–74 coup d'état] but sends television cameras and reporters instead. These days democracy rules with power of its own propoganda.'[12] CCF's point was to show 'the upgraded role of the journalists' and their collusion with the mainstream parties in manipulating the country's institutions for their own benefit. 'In the democracy of our time', the group asserted, 'the media have taken on the role of middlemen, which explains why an ever increasing number of staffing of political offices is filled by former high-profile journalists. It is all part of democracy's advanced communication strategy.'[13]

The main weight of the communiqué, however, fell on CCF's scathing attack on the Greek electorate, 'the masses'. CCF painted a condescending picture of a naive, chronically spineless and defeatist electorate. History alone, the group said, has proven that 'one should have no confidence' whatsoever in the opinion of 'the masses': 'They who voluntarily adopt for themselves the term "people" and speak as part of "we the people", instead of taking their fates into their own hands, abandon all creative self-confidence and let themselves believe in the fallacy of their leaders.'[14] This is the people, the group went on: 'a noisy mass with lowered heads, incessant moaning, misery and crowd mentality that degrades life into a repeated operation and adherence to rules. There is no good reason for us to respect either its judgement or its choices.'[15]

The communiqué ended with a solidarity greeting to 17N's Koufodinas,[16] imprisoned in 'democracy's white cells', and a sneer at the police apparatus for exaggerating the significance of a CCF safe-house raid four months earlier in the northern suburb of Halandri that resulted in the arrests of four CCF militants.[17] Ridiculing the police operation as 'a spectacular fiesta', CCF pointed to the fact that although several months had gone by after their 'supposed dismantling', they remained manifestly active. The group paid tribute to the arrested militants,[18] reiterating at the same time their total commitment to their cause. 'Our organization', the group asserted, 'suffered no blow whatsoever; on the contrary, we are constantly strengthened in the context of revolutionary potentiality of the present. In any case our actions speak for themselves. To [your] democracy we shall show no respect, only rage and attack.'[19]

CCF's Parcel Bomb Campaign

On 1 November 2010, a parcel addressed to the Mexican embassy in Athens exploded in the headquarters of a courier company, injuring the employee who handled it. Soon after the blast the police arrived on the scene and managed to catch up with the assailants, using physical descriptions given by witnesses at the courier company. The two men, who turned out to be CCF militants already wanted by the police, had both been wearing bullet-proof vests and carrying Glock 9 mm pistols and rucksacks that contained two more parcel bombs addressed to the French President Nicolas Sarkozy and the Belgian embassy in Athens respectively. Their arrests, however, did nothing to prevent the two-day barrage of parcel bombings (fourteen in total) that followed. The group targeted several embassies, including those of Switzerland, Russia and Chile, throughout Athens and the offices of President Sarkozy, the German Chancellor Angela Merkel and the Italian Prime Minister Silvio Berlusconi, forcing the Greek government to suspend overseas shipment of mail and packages for forty-eight hours.

While the Greek government denounced CCF's campaign as 'mindless and irresponsible, aimed at damaging the country's efforts to put the economy back on track and regain credibility',[20] the group released a nineteen-page communiqué entitled 'Announcement Regarding our Arrested Comrades'. The text paid tribute, in a rather melodramatic style, to the imprisoned CCF members for their 'uncompromising attitude', declaring, at the same time, the group's determination to continue their activity both inside and outside prison. 'From this point on', the text said in an introductory paragraph that was meant to provide gravitas, CCF's agenda would be:

> expressed through two independent and equal infrastructures: we, who now designate ourselves as the illegal sector of the organization and the other, the nucleus of the imprisoned members of the organization (Gerasimos Tsakalos, Panagiotis Argyrou, Charis Chatzimihelakis). Henceforth, their word is also our word and their decisions represent us too. We shall do our best to live up to their expectations and to honour their confidence in us.[21]

Although entitled 'Announcement Regarding our Arrested Comrades' the bulk of the communiqué was primarily devoted to the identity consolidation of the external group instead of examining how a CCF prison sector would continue the struggle from inside the prison. In the past, imprisoned members of European revolutionary groups such as the Italian Red Brigades and the German Red Army Faction, would conduct occasional hunger strikes, make ideological pronouncements and submit tactical proposals in order to 'mobilize' both the commando and sympathizer levels.[22]

A mixture of political commentary and rebellious defiance, 'Announcement Regarding our Arrested Comrades' represented a CCF attempt to reiterate its revolutionary optimism, organizational continuity and commitment to the armed struggle. CCF also stated that its organizational genesis derived from 'a new wave of revolutionary anarchy that had forcefully and dynamically entered the field of social conflict'.[23] Attacking state mechanisms, finance capitalism and left-wing reformism, CCF reaffirmed its ambition to be a leading 'part of the militant anarchy of the new urban guerrilla movement that exercised incessant armed criticism of the tyranny of those "on the top" but also to the compromises made by those beneath'.[24] This last point raised the question of how weak and inadequate the level of opposition had been on part of the Greek populace in responding to power elites and state oppression. No wonder, CCF said, the future of 'this crowd of complacent citizens' was sealed.[25] The 'acceptance and resignation' of what the CCF contemptuously called 'the silent crowd' not only made things easy for state capitalism and its representatives but it also undermined any serious development of a culture of resistance.[26]

Moving on to the financial crisis and its consequences afflicting Greek society, CCF said that economic misery combined with existing social injustice, environmental degradation and the stress of urban life had all 'formed a frame of social cannibalism'.[27] CCF attributed Greece's economic ills to worldwide factors, adding that 'the repeated blows of the financial crisis had virtually destroyed the social consensus that was built around the consumer ideal and the promise of continuous material well-being'.[28] 'The culture of easy, quick money', CCF added, and of 'a corresponding social advancement was now giving way to backward situations of economic deprivation.'[29] Against that background, CCF said in a matter-of-fact tone, Greece, given its continuing economic slide, would become a theatre of great conflicts. 'The only question now', CCF said, 'is which side will everyone choose?'[30]

The group made no bones about the route it had chosen to follow even if it ultimately meant going it alone. CCF writers said that 'everyone has to make their own choices and be judged by them. This is why through our texts we frequently promote the anarchist-individualist perception as a new pattern of behaviour and a motif for action.'[31] This does not mean', CCF added, 'that we are not interested in opening dialogue with other people. We, in fact, expect and welcome any criticism that would set us to thinking and make us better.'[32] However, CCF added, 'we are not going to wait for social approval in order to act. We are unwilling wait for the conditions to "mature". If society does not understand our ideas, then the problem is with society … But one thing is for certain', the group said: 'we are done waiting in the wings.'[33]

In the same emphatic mode, CCF writers sought to show that that their use of 'revolutionary violence' was effectively an 'eye-to-eye' response against 'state barbarity' and terror rather than terrorism.[34] By reasoning in the same way that other Greek revolutionary groups had done previously, the group said that 'considering the terror exercised by those "on top" with wars, poverty, labour accidents, police, prisons, there must be a response to the terror with terror from the "bottom"'.[35] And even then, CCF said, 'the guerrilla violence of an explosive device or a political execution cannot be compared with the genocides and murders carried out by the state though it is a small transfer of terror to the enemy camp.' The fact that 'all these bastards who dominate our lives are bound to move around in armoured cars accompanied by small armies of bodyguards because of our actions is the minimum price they have to pay for the world they have built to govern'.[36]

In the final section of 'Announcement Regarding our Arrested Comrades' CCF stressed its commitment and determination to advance the revolutionary cause internationally. For the revolution to survive, CCF said, it needed to spread internationally. It was now imperative, the group added, that 'a new phase in the development of revolutionary thought and action was launched, a qualitative leap that would bring common choices, that are hundreds of thousands of kilometres away, a step closer'.[37] The group implicitly believed that 'a non-formalistic antiauthoritarian network of international guerrilla groups and autonomous individuals' would help to crystallize revolutionary strategy and tactics. Determined to make 'an international call in the coming months', CCF saw the network not merely as a starting point of an extended circle of communication, discussion, perception and reflection but also as a platform for coordinating attacks at an international level, exchanging material and technical knowledge in the field of sabotage and setting up an infrastructure for supporting imprisoned comrades and wanted revolutionaries.[38]

CCF ended the communiqué with a short summary of the prison community and prisoner support initiatives. Referring specifically to their 'own losses', CCF stressed that their own imprisoned members would neither be victimized nor mythologized.[39] Releasing them, CCF said, would take effort and time but the group promised to respond. Using the IRA's most famous prisoner Bobby Sands's cry of 'our day will come, our day will come', CCF said that it might be a slow, inch-by-inch struggle to remedy tangible injustices and transform degraded conditions, but the boot was now on the other foot. 'We as revolutionaries', CCF said, 'may have experienced the loss of our comrades, the imprisonment of our brothers, the manhunt from our persecutors but the time has come for the pain and the agony to change camps. Our day will come.'[40]

The Athens Court Building Attack

CCF ended 2010 with a major attack. On 30 December, a powerful bomb hidden on a parked motorcycle exploded outside a court building in the densely populated area of Ambelokipi, near central Athens. The rush-hour blast occurred at 8:20 a.m., following a warning telephone call to the *Eleftherotypia* newspaper and a TV station, shattering windows and nearby shop storefronts in a 200-meter radius, and seriously damaging at least ten cars. A mixture of ammonium nitrate and fuel oil (ANFO and TNT, used in construction but also in improvised explosive devices), the bomb was stored in a hard luggage case at the back of a stolen motorcycle.[41] There were no injuries but the explosion sent up a cloud of smoke that was visible across the city for hours.

Signed Conspiracy of Cells of Fire—*Commando Horst Fantazzini*,[42] the group said in a communiqué that the attack had been staged to express solidarity with the thirteen arrested members of CCF who were to face trial in January 2011.[43] The text was underpinned by the double theme of justice and imprisonment. Justice, according to CCF was 'a spider's web, catching small prey and swallowing them, while allowing at the same time big reptiles to penetrate and dominate'.[44] How could it not be so, the group added, considering that justice always had 'a special preference for uniforms, for authority and for money but not for truth'.[45]

In the same pugnacious prose, CCF writers took up the second theme of the communiqué, namely prisons and prisoners in Greece. The greatest threat to freedom, CCF said, was not violent deprivation through captivity, because the prisoner can fight to win that back. The real threat, the group said, was:

> the loss of the passion and appreciation you have for it. In prison what kills even more than smack is habit. The habit of wearing invisible handcuffs on your mind, the habit of the exercise yard, the surprise checks and transfers, the visits behind Plexiglas, the television which is permanently on.[46]

CCF believed implicitly that the Greek prison system was built on brutal oppression and exploitation and the only way to uproot and get rid of the oppression and exploitation was through protest, disruption and sabotage. The group used the maximum security Korydallos prison, where most 17N, RS and the recently arrested CCF militants were held, as an example. Korydallos, said the group, had about '2,500 inmates guarded by no more than fifty on-duty screws. If all these inmates refused to cooperate with these fifty individuals, refused to play the game with the carrot and the stick, they could then tear the prison down overnight.'[47]

The group saved its most intimidating vocabulary until the end of the communiqué to castigate the 'corrupt judicial mafia' for its role in the forthcoming trial of their comrades. 'Since you are not ashamed', the group said:

> to be the spearhead of the system against the coming insurgencies, we will make sure that you feel our dislike and disgust for your dirty work. If some of you consider that you're only doing your job by judging ideas and prosecuting revolutionaries, then we'll make sure that we do our own job too.[48]

CCF ended its communiqué vowing to avenge the imprisonment of its members. 'Modern-day inquisitors-judges, we publicly pledge that for every year of prison that our brothers receive, we shall put a kilo of explosives in your front yards, in your cars, in your offices, while we don't exclude any face-to-face meetings with you.'[49] The world, CCF said meaningfully, was a small place and 'sooner or later we will meet again'.[50]

CCF in Prison

The histories of several European terrorist organizations have shown that groups such as the Italian BR, the German RAF and the French AD had all developed an active and dedicated prison sector that continued the armed struggle from inside the prisons. The primary functions of the RAF prison sector, for example, were to maintain group discipline and cohesion and to conduct occasional hunger strikes to mobilize the commando and resistance levels. Similarly, in the Italian Red Brigades, prison was seen as an alternative battleground to continue the struggle. In fact, imprisoned brigadisti were responsible for ensuring consolidation of the group's collective identity inside as well as for discussing strategy and making tactical proposals for submission to the group's external leadership. In the case of the IRA prison sector, even a journal was produced quarterly by the prisoners under the name of *An Glor Gafa* (The Captive Voice).

The Greek terrorist prison experience, until the emergence of CCF, had been virtually non-existent. With the exception of 17N's head of operations Koufodinas,[51] who continues to this day to assert his political status and resist state criminalization through sporadic hunger strikes and protestations against prison rules and procedures, 'the revolutionary spirit' of the rest of the imprisoned 17N group members quickly evaporated. Like other prisoners from European revolutionary groups in the past, the CCF prisoners considered themselves a part of the resistance and saw prison as the final front of their struggle.[52] Led by Gerasimos Tsakalos, Panagiotis Argyrou and Charis Chatzimichelakis, the 'Nucleus of the Imprisoned Members of the Organization', as it was called, was fully and publicly supported by the CCF commando level who, in a communiqué, stated that 'their word is also our word while their decisions represent us too'.[53] In a series of letters, announcements and other initiatives, the CCF prison sector were determined to show that 'even in captivity they have reversed the terms of a defeatist capitulation and have proudly taken responsibility for their actions, defending the positions and values of CCF'.[54]

Gerasimos Tsakalos

Born into a relatively well off family, the twenty-four year old (at the time of his arrest in November 2010 in Pangrati after attempting to mail package-bombs to various embassies) Tsakalos never seemed to hold any steady jobs and he and his brother, also a CCF militant, lived by renting out properties inherited from his father, a talented and well-known song lyricist.

Writing from Korydallos prison, before a quick succession of moves to Maladrinos and Domokos prisons, Tsakalos describes in one of his several letters the first days after his arrest and the treatment he received at the hands of the Greek counter-terrorist unit. 'Holding the obvious attitude that every revolutionary should have', he wrote, 'we refused to have our fingerprints, photographs and DNA taken and generally refused to sign anything or help these pigs in the least.'[55] Tsakalos painted a picture of a panicky group of counter-terrorist officers who became incensed by his total lack of cooperation. 'Our negative attitude to their questioning', he wrote:

> combined with the fact that there were still bomb parcels being delivered out there infuriated them. As their stress and anxiety increased, so did their threats: first they talked about executing me on Imitos mountain and then how they would throw me out of the window if there was any problem with the plane that carried the letter-bomb [sent to Italian PM Silvio Berlusconi] in Italy.[56]

Tsakalos went further declaring that:

> all this is not reported from the viewpoint of a victim of police violence, since I do not feel at all like this, but in order to share some personal experiences so when a fighter does have an "unlucky" moment he has a better picture of the situation he will be confronted with.[57]

Anxious not to present himself in heroic terms, he quickly added that 'threats and violence from the police were to be expected. Compared to the severe torture thousands of prisoners have suffered in police stations everywhere, their treatment towards me looks civilized.'[58] For Tsakalos there was little doubt: there were no good cops and bad cops, there were only cops and the revolutionary organizations had to attack them with all means.

Advocating 'revolutionary nihilism' and 'anarchist anti-socialism', Tsakalos deplored all those individuals in positions of power, calling them 'a pile of creeps, liars, frauds and sadists' who kept taking a series of devastating decisions for everyone.[59] Yet the question Tsakalos posed was:

> Who votes them in? Who respects them by bowing their heads? Who admires them and wants to be like them? Who keeps quiet in front of the gross injustices they commit? The answer is easy: Society. Society selected them in the first place and it gave them power to take decisions on its behalf. And if we were to accept that everyone is entitled to a mistake, making the same mistake over and over again, seems to me deliberate.[60]

Tsakalos's most zealous attacks, however, were directed against certain parts of the anarchist movement that had been critical towards the group itself. Calling them 'hyenas of solidarity', Tsakalos took issue with the way they, 'this dreary minority which like permanent thorns damages the movement and its processes',[61] handled the 5 May 2010 arson incident at the Marfin Bank in which three bank employees lost their lives.[62] Although Tsakalos conceded that 'the arson of the bank was executed in the worst possible way and led to the unfortunate result of three deaths', the CCF militant was dismissive of the way certain 'anarcho-patriarchs' had taken advantage of a bad situation to target the new generation of the anarchist movement. Tsakalos saw the Marfin Bank incident as an issue with major ideological implications for the future direction of the movement. His, and by implication CCF's, position was clear enough: 'Those very few comrades left who still want to be like them, they should fuck off and give space to a lot of new individuals with a healthy way of thinking and the revolutionary dignity to act.'[63] Tsakalos ended his letter by paying his 'respects to the 17N guerrillas and other political hostages whose dignity guides our steps'.[64]

The Seven Days Hunger Strike

On 3 February 2011, four CCF prisoners began a hunger strike in protest against the authorities' decision to have the visitors to the public gallery of Korydallos court have their identification cards retained by the police and for the court proceedings not to be recorded (the procedure had been foregone to save on expenses). In a letter signed by Charis Chadjimihelakis Panagiotis Argirou, Panagiotis Masouras and Giorgos Karagiannidis, CCF prisoners said that they had reached the decision to 'escalate their mobilization, going from abstention from prison food to hunger strike' until their demands were met.[65] In an abrasive style, CCF prisoners said a point had been reached where they would not back off from certain things: 'we do not ask, we demand that they [the court authorities] do not register all those comrades or relatives and friends interested in being near us at this moment. The recognition of their contribution is essential and the significance of their solidarity and support cannot but oblige us to rise to the occasion'.[66] In fact, CCF prisoners took the view that their hunger strike reached a deeper level than a political dispute with the court authorities as their prison struggle could set a benchmark for the future. 'Given the character of our trial and the fact that these politically motivated measures were taken by the court in a clear attempt to terrorize the people in solidarity', the CCF prisoners said that their actions carried wider implications for all the trials of such nature that were bound to follow.[67]

However, a week later, on 11 February 2011, the four CCF prisoners released 'an announcement' ending their hunger strike. In an attempt to pre-empt any possible backlash from the wider anarcho-leftist movement, the CCF letter went to great lengths to explain their sudden U-turn, providing a detailed picture of their legal manoeuvres and obstructionist tactics (refusal to turn up in court and dismissal of three set of lawyers) to keep the trial suspended until their demands were met. 'We know', CCF wrote in an apologetic tone, that 'such actions and forms of struggle leave their prints on the history of the revolutionary subversive movement and hence have a public character and are exposed to any criticism'.[68] 'Considering', CCF went on, 'that we are stopping the strike before our demands are satisfied and a very short time after it began, we decided to make a public statement carrying out an assessment of our mobilisation from the beginning of the trial until now.'[69]

CCF's 'mobilisation assessment' offered in fact a glimpse of the internal group dynamics among the CCF militants inside prison as debates and disagreements over tactics were aired. The text placed a lot of emphasis on 'the regression' of fellow prisoner Konstandina Karakatsani who, according to the CCF four not only opposed the decision to go on hunger strike but was also unwilling to join the rest of the group in their legal obstructionisms. Discussing Karakatsanis's attitude, apparent lack of commitment to the cause and reluctance to be part of a united front, the CCF four painted a picture of a selfish comrade whose opportunism compromised the entire effort.

'When a person and especially an anarchist', they explained, 'makes agreements they should keep their word, particularly when these agreements involve consequences, not only for them, but also for the rest as well.'[70] However, what 'enraged' the CCF four more than Karakatsanis's decision 'to split a fighting front that could have achieved an important victory against the court' was her 'attempts to wrap the regression in a political cloak'.[71]

Overall, the 'Announcement' was an exercise in self-justification but also an indirect mea culpa on the part of the CCF four for failing to recognize that prison struggle was far from straightforward. 'Self-criticism is a weapon for every revolutionary', the CCF letter said, 'and in this context we recognize our error to support the whole process on an agreement that was not based on a common consensus, since all of us are disparate individuals with different starting lines of struggle, political attitudes, convictions and perceptions.'[72]

Konstantina Karakatsani

Born in 1991, in Paleo Faliro, Konstantina 'Nina' Karakatsani left the family home at the age of seventeen, which is very early by any standards, let alone Greek standards. Before she became a fugitive in September 2009, she was working as a tattoo designer and was romantically involved with two CCF militants, first with Nikos Vogiatzakis and then with Giorgos Nikolopoulos. Incriminated by fingerprints found in the Halandri safe house, Karakatsanis was eventually arrested in April 2010 although she denied any involvement in the group.[73]

While on the run Karakatsanis became a cause celebre in Greek extra-parliamentary circles because of a letter she sent to *Eleftherotypia* in which, full of contempt, she attacked the police and the then Minister of Public Order Michalis Chrysochoidis for fabricating evidence incriminating the people involved in the Halandri safe-house case. In her polemics against the Minister and the security apparatus, Karakatsani contended that 'they decided to label the house "a safe-house", the gathering "an organization" and the individuals visiting the house "ruthless terrorists" in a desperate attempt to show that they were making some kind of progress'.[74] Ridiculing police calls for her to turn herself in, Karakatsanis explained that this was not going to happen for the simple reason that she 'did not want to end up in jail because someone decided that the cells of their democracy had space left to be filled'.[75] 'What will come next is for them to link us to al-Qaeda', she added sarcastically.[76] However, the letter's ultimate purpose was to assert her political identity while at the same time vindicating her readiness to go against the state's security apparatus and judicial mechanisms. 'Why should I turn myself in?' she asked rhetorically. 'Should I just go so I can prove that I'm not an elephant? What is there exactly for me to negotiate? I am an anarchist, not a beggar to be begging and haggling.'[77]

Like her letter to *Eleftherotypia*, Karakatsanis's writings from prison were equally characterised by abrasive eloquence and belligerence. In a six-page letter-response to the CCF four, Karakatsanis dismissed the accusations of 'regression', deploring at the same time the moralistic tone and polemical excess of their arguments. To Karakatsanis it was axiomatic that a response had to be made not because of political aggravation or frustration but in order 'to be consistent in your commitment to the wider struggle'.[78] Dealing with the question of whether she had 'supposedly' made 'an agreement' with her co-defendants, Karakatsanis said that it should have become obvious right from the start that she was 'handling this case alone' given that she did not 'align' herself with any texts or statements made by the others.[79] Not that her support was deemed necessary, she added, somewhat sarcastically, since 'some of them seemed determined to turn the trial into a spectacular blockbuster, one way or another'.[80] Reflecting on the hunger strike issue, Karakatsanis wanted to leave her readers in no doubt that she was opposed to the idea from the very beginning. Rigorously exploring the question of why a hunger strike 'placed on the wrong basis', would never achieve its end, Karakatsanis attacked her comrades for petulance and bloody-mindedness.[81] 'The state', she said in a matter-of-fact tone, 'is pressured by those who strike, not by those eating.' When these individuals realised', she said, 'that their choice wouldn't work out, they looked for an excuse to retreat and found it in me.'[82] As Karakatsani went on to explain, it was very easy to get lost in the intricacies of the argument, but the fact remained that:

> a hunger strike is not a simple painless instrument but a means of struggle in which the health and life of those who decide to use it is compromised. Alive or Dead. Either a winner standing or a loser lying down. A middle situation does not exist and no Karakatsani can be an excuse to retreat.[83]

Karakatsani was unequivocal about her comrades' intentions: 'when they got trapped by their wrong decision and had to face up to the responsibilities of their choices, they attempted to damage my moral and political credibility in order to retain theirs intact'.[84]

Karakatsanis's critical barrage towards her comrades and co-defendants ended with a sneer:

> I am and will remain INCONSISTENT for those who trivialize practices and demean forms of struggle that have historically been landmarks of struggles in revolutionary processes. INSINCERE for those who shift responsibilities to others, relegating even any sense of self-criticism. I am and always will be DISRUPTIVE for those who choose moves that are on the verge of self-victimization and give reasons to useless subjects to speak of me politically, who sabotage the revolutionary vision more efficiently than dominance itself. And honourably, I am and will be in the future ENRAGED towards those who adopt attitudes and behaviours that are not recognized within the scope of my political assessment. Among other things, I will also be a traitor to anything that does not coincide with my values and fighting positions.[85]

Karakatsanis was sentenced to eleven years in prison for 'belonging to a criminal organization' and 'for manufacturing and possessing explosives', as well as for complicity in the bomb attack against the house of PA.SO.K. minister Louka Katseli. Soon after the court handed down the jail terms, Karakatsanis's father, in a letter posted to the athensindymedia.org website, attacked 'PA.SO.K.'s justice which with no substantiated evidence and without taking into consideration her young age, condemned her. She is probably the world's youngest political prisoner.'[86]

The Second Period of CCF

CCF was a product of its environment. CCF's political physiognomy, the timing of its emergence and the logic behind the group's selection of targets can be explained by the radical and rapid changes in Greece's social, political and economic landscape. CCF, like all organizations which resort to terrorism, claimed that its cause justified extremism. Narrating its discourse through attack communiqués, announcements and interventions, CCF tried to elaborate the presentation of sociopolitical events, expanding the dimensions of their violent context in an attempt to dramatize the anomalies of the existing system, deny its legitimacy and propound alternative models. National public life was the most significant basis for CCF extremism. CCF's repeated references to liberal capitalism, the IMF, financial scandals, crises of governability and political corruption revealed its intense hostility towards national institutions, international interdependence, and transnational policies.

CCF's campaign of violence was centrally driven by a rejection of the values of the society in which it lived. The absolute nature of CCF's rejection recapitulates some elements of Sergei Nechaev's nihilism and helped to shape the group's overall worldview. Like Nechaev, CCF viewed revolution in terms of images: the future, hope, and the people.[87] It saw revolution as the only valid motive for action and the sole justification for armed militancy and violence. As its campaign grew more violent, the group repeatedly endorsed the claim that armed struggle was the only activity which could actually transform conditions. At the same time, CCF intended to embody the most elevated principles of protest action in what it saw as a critical moment for the anarchist-revolutionary movement. To prevent various organizations within the movement from prevaricating over the question of what level of violence was appropriate at the given historical juncture, CCF positioned itself as a pivotal element within the movement and began to practice 'vanguard violence'.

CCF's membership profile and political behaviour suggest a new generation of militants dissimilar in many respects from the older, highly-organized and mission-orientated metropolitan guerrillas of 17N. Born into middle class, relatively well-off families, educated in good schools and very young in age (the oldest thirty-two-years old), the personal histories of CCF militants illustrate the complex and unique ways in which people come to be involved in terrorism. CCF also illustrates that the younger and larger the group membership in a terrorist organization, the greater the likelihood for mistakes of a procedural and operational nature. Regular violations of basic conspiratorial rules and procedures by CCF militants in the first period (using mobile phones, keeping incriminating materials where they lived and being conspicuously involved in protests) cost the group dearly. However, the numerous arrests of key militants between 2009–2010 failed to destroy CCF. Conversely, the group seems to have constructed an effective enough support and sympathizer network to serve as a reserve manpower pool for the commando level which explains the emergence of a successor group in the summer of 2011 calling itself the second period of CCF.[88] It is impossible at this stage to estimate the current membership of the second period CCF but the group has embraced the view of the original CCF that only 'the continuation of revolutionary war' could raise awareness of the infrastructure of society and ignite social polarization. In an attack communiqué claiming responsibility for the firebombing of twelve Greek Telecom vehicles in July 2011, the group said that 'new guerrilla methodologies, infrastructures and battle tactics were already in the laboratory of the revolutionary development' and promised to be 'more dangerous, more unpredictable and more chaotic' than its predecessor.[89]

8

CONCLUSION

> Does the end justify the means? That is possible. But what will justify the end?
>
> Albert Camus, *The Rebel*

What can you do as a writer, Basque scholar Joseba Zulaika wondered, 'when your primary community of family, friends, village, or country produces "terrorists"? Is it your intellectual challenge to define them, diagnose them, condemn them, understand them, exorcize them?'[1] Having been researching Greek terrorism and political violence for the past twenty years, my main impetus for writing this book came from the deepening realization that the Greek terrorist landscape, in spite of 17N's spectacular demise, remains as enduring, complex and unpredictable as ever. This environment reflects an expanding terrain upon which violent extremist ideas continue to travel at great speed within Greek society, producing sociocultural enclaves whose commitment to democratic values and practices of representative politics can be characterized as problematic at best.

Campaigns of terrorism are not free-standing social phenomena. They depend on context, on circumstances—historical, political, social and economic—and on how groups and individuals conducting their violent campaigns relate to the societies within which they deploy force. Dealing primarily with Greece, this book has been written in the belief that—whether one supports politically motivated violence or not as a tactic—it is important to place the phenomenon in a clear frame of understanding and to attempt to explain why violent revolutionary organizations continue to emerge within certain democratic national settings. Regrettably, the only conclusion one can safely reach is that Greece has one of the most sustained problems of political terrorism anywhere in Europe. Even more unpalatable is the fact that there is nothing in view to indicate an escape route from what has become a permanent fixture of Greek contemporary life.

The collapse of Greece's premier terrorist organization, the 17 November group, back in the summer of 2002 was a truly dramatic event, considering 17N's twenty-seven-year career, but it was not quite the watershed event in the country's history that was presented at the time by the mainstream political and media establishments. 17N's dismantling and imprisonment, far from demoralizing and emasculating the armed struggle movement led to the emergence of new urban guerrilla groups and the increase and intensification of revolutionary violence.

As far as Greek terrorism is concerned, stereotypes continue to dominate much of the understanding of the various political organizations, old and new: their members are treated as politicized criminals and their use of violence as deviant/criminal behaviour, disregarding the country's larger revolutionary culture and the wider political and socioeconomic conditions that facilitate it.[2] It should come as little surprise that the trials of 17N and ELA[3] terrorist organizations, where the standard rules of procedure in the Greek judicial process for criminal cases were followed, failed to produce complete answers to critical questions,[4] and many aspects of the case remained unclear.[5] In the words of a senior Greek judge, who wished to remain anonymous, 'a great opportunity was lost'.[6]

Militants do not come out of nowhere, especially in a country with as complex and turbulent a history as Greece.[7] When a terrorist campaign begins, there is a reason for every bombing, every shooting and every rocket attack. In Greece, however, it has always been easier and more politically convenient for successive governments to think of terrorism simply as an unfortunate aberration or a fringe phenomenon, rather than to accept the fact that 'terrorist action is conducted in historical time by subjects who have been shaped and transformed by powerful political consequences'.[8] My research on the new generation of Greek militants confirms that post-17N terrorism derived directly from the presence of ideologies that justify violence. Ideas sustained by extreme-left traditions shaped, facilitated and oriented the political actions and strategies of the new groups. The evolution of RS and CCF show, in fact, how ideologically motivated political factions broke away from the larger, non-violent movement to which they were linked by modes of argumentation and forms of practice in order to 'become entrepreneurs of violence'.[9] Having rejected the very nature of Greek democracy, these newly emergent radical organizations escalated their demands symbolically, with the elaboration of distinctive frames of revolutionary rhetoric, and operationally, with the promotion of clandestine systematic violence.

Like their predecessors, the new generation of Greek terrorist groups did not use violence in the Clausewitzean sense of warlike pressure, namely that 'if our opponent is to be made to comply with our will, we must place him in a situation which is more oppressive to him than the sacrifice which we demand'.[10] The new groups both intoned the claims and revisited the martyrdoms and sacrifices of their predecessors. Both RS and CCF presented themselves and their violence in terms of solidarity, continuity and humanity. The groups embraced the belief that 'violence was not merely an instrumental technique for damaging opponents but also the symbolic basis of the community of activists'.[11] At the same time, their determination to link themselves to a broader level of social conflict was demonstrated in the choice of their targets. Both RS and CCF struck at symbols which they believed if damaged would humiliate the Greek political establishment, arouse popular protest and create revolutionary impetus. Through lengthy attack communiqués and strategic texts, the new groups elaborated the presentation of political events and expanded the dimensions of their violent context in an attempt to dramatize the anomalies of the existing system, deny its legitimacy and propound alternative models.

Regressively fixated on the memory of 17N, both groups, RS in particular, saw their violence as a historical extension of 17N's revolutionary grand narrative. Believing that 17N's revolutionary experiment could only be surpassed by a new revolutionary experiment, RS's overriding objective was to 'shape a genuine revolutionary current, equal to the requirements of the age'.[12] In that sense, RS embraced 17N's view of terrorist violence as a legitimate and logical form of expression for those humiliated and ridiculed by the ruthless capitalist mechanisms of power. RS, like all organizations which resort to terrorism, claimed that its cause justified extremism and the use of violence to intervene in Greek public life.

The second group of the new generation of Greek militants under examination, CCF, embraced revolutionary guerrilla warfare but unlike RS did not attempt to fit itself into Greek left-wing political traditions by formulating class-based criticisms of the Greek state. Viewing itself as 'anarcho-revolutionary', the CCF justified its campaign of terrorism with an ideology that largely resembled radical anarcho-communist traditions. 'Striking at the ordinary flow of the system', CCF's violence was intended to compensate for the coercive character of capitalism and modern mechanisms of dominant political and financial interests. The CCF's membership profile and political behaviour also suggested a new generation of militants dissimilar in many respects from the old-fashioned and mission-orientated metropolitan guerrillas of 17N. The CCF's campaign of violence was centrally driven by a rejection of the values of the society in which it lived. As its campaign grew more violent, the group repeatedly endorsed the 17N claim that armed struggle was the only activity which could actually transform conditions. At the same time, the CCF intended to embody the most elevated principles of protest action in what it saw as a critical moment for the Greek anarchist-revolutionary movement.

One of the central arguments of this study is that any serious examination of terrorist violence must deal not only with specific political factions, themes and influences but also with individual life histories in order to explore 'the interior views of those engaging in violence, tracing their evolution, claims, purposes and aims'.[13] As the chapters on the terrorist biographies have shown, Greek militants, 'normal and rational as other political actors tend to be' resorted to revolutionary militancy out of political choice and for their own private political ends.[14] One might argue that biographical recollections can be limiting because they provide a biased description of reality, offering the participants preferred images and perceptions of events. However, while it may be true that participants in terrorism can often have selective memory, using retrospective reasoning to justify or even beautify their actions, biographical accounts do 'allow us to reconstruct the movement milieus, the perceptions of the external worlds diffused among militants, their definition of the costs and benefits of participation, their political socialization, and the dynamic of producing and sustaining identity'.[15] At the same time, taking into account what the individual young militants have to say about their own personal reactions and experiences from involvement in terrorist activity also furthers our understanding of terrorist recruitment practices, group dynamics and commitment mechanisms.

A central factor in determining the longevity of terrorist political violence lies in the degree of commitment and the beliefs of those involved. One of the reasons why ELA's and 17N's campaigns endured so long, apart from the Greek state's incompetence in diagnosing the problem early on, was because of the genuine political commitment of the militants involved. Carlos Marighela, the Brazilian Marxist revolutionary and author of the *Minimanual of the Urban Guerrilla*, contended that it was 'moral superiority' which sustained most armed guerrilla movements and the Greek terrorist experience confirms this belief.[16] 17N's chief of operations Dimitris Koufodinas portrayed the Greek armed revolutionary as someone 'whose life choices are actually made against his personal interests'.[17] A revolutionary, he said, 'if he is true to himself and to his ideas has the obligation to go all the way'.[18] Unlike the Maoist Shining Path (Sendero Luminoso) leader Abimael Guzman who, after his dramatic arrest in 1992, wrote letters from prison to fellow Sendero activists, urging them to lay down their arms and use non-violent methods, Koufodinas remained committed to violence as a method of achieving social and political change. As long as groups like 17N 'intervened' and 'resisted', Koufodinas told the perplexed president of the court, it did not matter that there might never be a military victory. For Koufodinas, who since his imprisonment has become an icon of the Greek armed struggle movement, what was and what remained important was the act of 'resistance'. Echoing this revolutionary brand of politics, Koufodinas's counterpart in ELA and the group's theoretician Christos Tsigaridas took the confident view that in Greece there would 'never be a shortage of armed revolutionary groups' and the total of sixty-four organizational acronyms that have appeared on the scene since the demise of his own organization back in 1996 prove that his optimism regarding the depth of Greece's revolutionary community was not baseless.[19] To men like Tsigaridas and Koufodinas, it was axiomatic that a revolutionary militant led from the front and always took political responsibility for his actions irrespective of the cost, a view shared by key personalities of the new generation of Greek revolutionaries such as Nikos Maziotis, the fugitive leader of RS.[20] It is a measure of Maziotis's absolute commitment to the cause that neither the decapitation of RS nor the birth of his own son, to his also imprisoned partner, made him reassess his life and choices. In fact, while in prison Maziotis painted a telling picture of the present-day Greek revolutionary militant when he insisted that becoming a father did not 'cancel out' the fact that he was also a member of 'an armed revolutionary organization'. 'As a matter of fact', he said:

> all our struggles take place so that we can hand over to our children a better world while making certain that we never place ourselves in the difficult position of having to admit to them when they grow up that we did nothing to resist the unfairness of the existing system.[21]

When the Korydallos prison authorities refused Maziotis visiting rights to the maternity hospital where his partner and RS comrade Panagiota Roupa was to give birth to their son because of 'security concerns', the RS militant went on hunger strike.[22]

One might, as one veteran Greek politician personally affected by terrorism did, dismiss Koufodinas, Tsigaridas and Maziotis as 'victims of romantic fanaticism',[23] pointing to the fringe status of the groups they led and the failure of those groups to affect the political order. However, a history of failure is not necessarily a history of insignificance. The extraordinary durability of ELA's and 17N's campaigns, and the subsequent dynamic emergence of a new generation of militant groups, reveal how the 'visibility of terrorism enhances its contagiousness'.[24]

Central to this book is the view that people in liberal democratic societies rarely choose to commit political violence without discourse. Terrorists, in other words, are made, not born. They need, as David Apter once put it, 'to talk themselves into it'.[25] Political choices are rooted in beliefs that are fundamental to society, and a belief in the utility and necessity of violence suggests systemic collective grievances as well as 'institutional weaknesses and blockages, or normative insufficiencies, injustices, or inequities, i.e. wrongs to be righted'.[26] Put differently, one does not have to be an apologist for Greek terrorism to recognize that many of the grievances of these organizations, old and new—abuse of authority, political corruption, police brutality—have been legitimate, concrete and far from slight.

Each society has its own mental inventory of patterns, symbols and images that are formed and preserved through long periods of time. In Greece, politico-ideological currents and principles stemming from mid-1970s radicalism remain alive today in a way that is difficult to imagine in other European countries with comparably developed radical intellectual and political cultures such as Italy or Spain. In Greek political culture, militant opposition and violent direct action against the established sociopolitical order continue to function as weapons of confrontation and disagreement by groups frustrated by what they perceive as an unresponsive political system. ELA and 17N were the first political organizations to present themselves in terms of political dissent, moral conviction and armed insurrection. Their successor groups, drawing upon the languages of political revolution and radical utopianism attempted to replicate what 17N's consistent, intransigent campaign tried and failed to do: to paralyse Greek public life and discredit the establishment.

Greek national institutions have proven resilient to and able to withstand intense levels of terrorist activity but it would be a mistake to underestimate the effects persistent violent campaigns can have on political attitudes and behaviour.[27] What became clear from the week-long street violence and small-scale terrorism of the December 2008 riots was the extent to which direct action and other expressions of political anger were widely shared across the spectrum of militant and political organizations and individuals.[28] The riots were not, as many claimed, an uprising or insurrection against the Greek government's neo-liberal economic policies.[29] Many of the measures deemed responsible for the violence had not even taken effect at the time when Athens was burning. Placing a politically convenient emphasis on their role masks the long-standing cultural factors and social deformities that lie beneath the violence.

This is not to say that the debt crisis, which continues to cast a dark cloud over the country, has not made matters worse. The signs of severe economic distress, deepening social polarization, uncontrolled immigration, disaffected policing and generalized anomie in the Greek capital in particular are too many and too visible to dismiss.[30] The fault lines in Greek society are deepening. Since May 2012, Greece has become the first European country to elect a neo-Nazi party, the racist Golden Dawn, to its parliament. Golden Dawn won votes across much of the country and not simply in inner cities where its supporters stage pogroms against immigrants and do battle with leftist youths and anarchists. What the rise of Golden Dawn confirms, in a country that has suffered so much at the hands of the Nazis and its own military junta, is that a divided and broken society now sits alongside the broken economy.[31]

Irrespective of its history and reputation, Greek democracy has not been functioning well. Episodes of dissent, disorder and violence, even terrorism, are part and parcel of every pluralistic political environment; but when terrorist activity becomes part of a nation's daily routine, as it has in Greece, democracy is put at unnecessary risk.

APPENDIX 1

Excerpts of Revolutionary Struggle communiqué sent to *Pontiki* weekly newspaper on 13 May 2004:

...According to this propaganda, it would appear that prosperity reigns in Greece; when 21 per cent of [its] people live on the poverty line, when unemployment is continuously on the increase, when 10,000 people in Athens are homeless. It would appear that we are living in a society of "equal" rights and opportunities, except that this condition relates to a handful of privileged persons, who reap the profits of the development programs, and the profitability and competitiveness of whose businesses reflect the "grandeur" of modern and powerful Greece.

The powerful Greece on a development path is in Sofokleous Street [the Athens Stock Exchange], where the big companies are reaping the super-profits of the stock-exchange gamble. The powerful Greece refers to the SEV [Greek Industrialists' Union] and the industrialists who since 1998 have pocketed three billion euros from subsidies, in the shape of developmental incentives. It refers to the state-paid employees of "Athens 2004" [Athens Olympics Organizing Committee] with salaries in the millions of euros, at a time when the basic salary is 500 euros, It refers to the businessmen participating in the materialization of the Olympic "vision", whose cost already has exceeded five billion euros. It refers to the large contracting companies that are profiting by the scandalous waste on the so-called development and Olympic projects. It refers to the government employees and their various collaborations with the economic crème de la crème of this land, an ongoing and daily phenomenon, which, whenever it is made public—because of mishandling by the persons involved—is condemned with repugnance as a political scandal.

This powerful Greece is being built at the expense of a majority, which is living under the daily terrorism of poverty, unemployment, over-indebtedness to the banking vampires. A majority which is not entitled to strike, since in the otherwise "free and democratic" environment strikes are criminalized and are prosecuted, one after the other, as illegal and abusive. A majority which continuously has to adapt to the requirements of the market and to accept without protest the elastified terms of employment, the privatization of the unemployed and the renting out of workers, through use of individual contracts extending up to a week. A majority which is forced to submit to businessmen's extortions over the widely-used solution of "moving" companies to countries with cheaper workforces, and to "make do" with the starvation wages which employers offer, in the name of increasing productivity.

This powerful and modern Greece is the Greece of the Riot Police [MAT], which attacks demonstrators, strikers and farmers. This powerful Greece is being built with the blood of dead workers, who from 1999 to date by far exceed 750, in a total of work-related accidents reaching 20,000. And because our "rule of law" state knows how to reward the regime's beasts of burden, it open-handedly gives pensions—to the survivors, of course—of less than 400 euros. This powerful Greece is being fed by the bleeding of immigrants, who are forced to live in modern-day slave trade conditions, most of them without social insurance putting in even sixteen hours [daily] on the large projects, and who are deported whenever the pace and the requirements of the Greek market dictate it. The achievements in security are measured by the numbers of the mutilated and dead immigrants at the minefields along the Evros [river, Greek-Turkish north-eastern border] and by the numbers of the drowned, which the Aegean waves wash ashore.

This powerful Greece is reflected in the Greek state's ability to acquire an increasingly centralized nature (which is happening in each state today), and to consolidate the regime's security and stability with the smallest possible social cost whenever necessary to impose occupation conditions ("red" zones in demonstrations), to imprison freedom and civil liberty fighters, to hold cities under police regime on a daily basis, to control, to try, to convict. The powerful and secure Greece is being built through the terrorism exercised to the detriment of the majority, by the oligarchy of the rich and the system's political administrators.

This reality is perpetuated and legitimized every four years through the elections. Social discontent is diminished to a certain extent, new futile hopes for a better future are raised in many through the change in party assuming power. However, once again, the belying is not long in coming. What the future holds is greater poverty, greater unemployment, more excluded and disenfranchised. These are the direct results of the policies of the new government, which will undertake to implement in Greece the economic plans of those who are powerful in Europe (Germany, France, England) in order to achieve the Lisbon targets. Harsher persecutions are expected of those who resist, demonstrate, strike. More prisons will be built. War conditions are expected to prevail throughout the country, with the contribution of other NATO armed forces in view of the Olympic Games, which have assumed the nature of an international military and police exercise for consolidating the regime's order and security. The powerful Greece of the future will be even more merciless than the Greece of today. And social indignation will seek the political terms to express itself, perhaps with greater severity that had so far been expressed.

Revolution Is the Only Way Out

An issue which arises is for how much longer this regime will be able to maintain control over a social situation of dubious stability. For how much longer will globalization constitute the "ideal" system "gifted by nature" to diffuse its contradictions, while the economic and political elites will have the opportunity to convince the people that the magical solution to the problem of unemployment and poverty lies in development. For how much longer will the modern dominators have the latitude to brag that neoliberal democracy is the most ideal political system, the definitive and irreversible conclusion of human political history. We believe that there are more than a few who acknowledge that objective conditions, such as they currently are and mainly, as they are taking shape, with the increasing aggravation of inequalities, more than justify the expression of mass social unrest aimed at overthrowing the system. Moreover, that there are more than a few who expect such developments.

To a great extent, preventing such a potential hinges on the ability of those in power to hinder the social base from becoming convinced that any collective attempt at changing living conditions is feasible; this is handled either through propoganda, which seeks either to eliminate or to isolate radical practices and theories, or through repression, in the cases in which dynamic practices of political challenges manifest. And because to a great extent the existing social and political crisis is reflected in the mass descent to the streets of individuals protesting against globalization, as is the case in international meetings, through its organizational structures the regime-aligned left wing undertakes to convert social challenge, grafting into it [the social crisis] ideologies which complement and support the regime, also channeling it into directions which are painless for the economic and political system. The effectiveness of the efforts of these left wing rearguards to capitalism, to "rationalize" the social crisis, placing it in the context of demands for reform, to a great extent relies on their ability to preserve and to disseminate to an increasing audience perceptions which argue for and promote a discrediting of revolutionary violence. And to this end they do not hesitate to condemn armed fighters and their choice to engage in armed struggle even when they are imprisoned in the regime's prisons.

For our part, we believe that the system of the modern globalized economic and political order is neither viable, nor does it have margins for improvement or effective reform. The over-concentration of social power in the hands of a minority and the increasing misery which besets the majority are not expressions of the unfortunate and extreme manifestations of the system, which otherwise—as many persons maintain, because of self-interest, without believing so—is "hopeful"; rather, they are expressions of the system's contemporary form, which competes with savage nineteenth century capitalism in barbarity.

Our only way out is to refuse to legitimize, through inactivity and through self-distancing, this system's crimes, to refuse to accept conditions of lack of freedom and of submission for ourselves. The "silent majority", which every four years votes but does not control in any way whatsoever, is the ideal ally of the rulers of any type, and social passivity is their ideal condition. So-called neutrality has a dynamic of its own, which the regime supports and nourishes. In reality, we all have two choices: either through our inactivity to strengthen the existing barbarity, or through action to cancel the system's "omnipotence", to rupture acquiescence, to dissipate social fear which today is the basic component of modern hegemony.

Let us once and for all reject views and perceptions which in any way support and justify this rotten regime. Let us line ourselves up against all those who believe that with thousands of protests we may resist the crimes being carried out against whole peoples—against us all—in the name of "counter-terrorism", let us prove how dangerous all those are who maintain all sorts of pacifist delusions and the unrealistic view that a peaceful resolution of political and social problems is feasible, within the framework of the current political form, which only euphemistically is termed a democracy. Let us line ourselves up against the apologists for regime morality and a bourgeois legitimacy, from whichever political area they may derive, who condemn armed action. Let us directly attack the mechanisms and the organizations which support the New [World] Order's crimes, capitalism's structures, both economic and political, as well as the state mechanism and its offshoots. Let us fight to reverse the terms of modern warfare, moving to counterattack, transferring fear to within the system and its servants. Let us fight to awaken consciences and to radicalize them, so as to formulate underlying conditions, to spread the struggle and revolutionary hope wide.

This is the direction towards which we believe it is worthwhile for one to struggle. For it is only in the continuous struggle towards a revolution that the field of true freedom currently lies. To create a world in which meanings such as equality and prosperity will not be a pipe-dream, in which the concept of progress will not be connected with the modern barbarity of high-technology, where it will signify society's ability to ensure equality of rights, each individual will have the freedom for self-determination and the ability to participate in the formulation of the social and economic organization. Such a world is attainable only within the framework of a society in which its structures do not favour the concentration of political and economic power in the hands of a few, but to the contrary, will exist in order to ensure that such phenomena do not reappear and that collective life will be co-administered horizontally. We believe that with such an international prospect, the realization of the revolutionary vision is possible and achievable. The true charge to heaven…

We assume responsibility for the bomb attack at the Evelpidon courthouse, on 5 September 2003. Moreover, we assume responsibility for the bomb attack on the Citibank branch at Neo Psychiko, on 14 March 2004.

APPENDIX 2

Excerpts of Conspiracy of Cells of Fire text posted on Athens Indymedia website on 25 November 2010:

At this point in time, three members of our organization are incarcerated in Greek democracy's prisons. Their absence from our side is not rectified through the text of a proclamation. Words seem hopelessly small and insignificant in the face of the intensity of the situations and of the emotions we have shared with them. Nevertheless even at these moments in time in which the prison walls and bars stand between us, nothing has changed. With their uncompromising attitude and their assumption of responsibility as members of the CCF Gerasimos Tsakalos, Panagiotis Argyrou and Charis Chatzimichelakis are giving the rest of us the signal for continuing the hostilities. In their pride we meet our own pride and in their smile our own smile.

In the past year and a half Panagiotis and Gerasimos, two of the most sincere and dignified rebels, had passed to the forefront of illegality having opted to be in a constant fighting stance towards the system and its toadies. In remand for a year and a half, and in order to protect his wider circle of friends from being targeted by the police (seventeen people in all were charged with participating in the Conspiracy because of fingerprints found at Charis's home), at first Charis denied the fact that he was a member of the organization. However, with the recent arrest of our two brothers, his honour and pride as a revolutionary led him to assume the political responsibility of participation in the Conspiracy.

We will not expand further. We do not like to be the ones talking about our brothers, we prefer to speak directly with them. For the time being we offer them our commitment ... We are not retreating ... we stand, do are not trying ... we can, we are not begging ... we rob, we are not erasing… we set ablaze, we are not awaiting … we look forward impatiently… The Conspiracy will never be arrested, because it is not merely an organization, it is a stream of ideas and ideas are always unarrestable… The date as yet has not been marked in the calendar. Every month, every week, every day they are always available. One of these days will be marked with a smile, the smile of our meeting again for continuing OUR adventure…

I) Truce? Never and nowhere.

"*Arm yourselves and become violent, beautifully violent, until everything is blown up. Because you should bear in mind that any violent action against the promoters of inequality is absolutely justified through the centuries of ceaseless violence we have received from them. Arm yourselves and fight state terrorism—burn, conspire, sabotage, and be violent, beautifully violent, physically violent, deliberately violent.*" Mauricio Morales [Urban guerrilla who was killed in Chile]

Let us shout loudly in the international language of revolution. Where words are pronounced differently, but confront common landscapes, without masters and slaves, without the tyranny of goods and images to govern us. Let our voices become a wind which will travel to where rebellion conspires. From the neighborhoods of Buenos Aires to the nights in Athens and Thessaloniki and from the cities of Chile and Mexico to the streets of France and Belgium. Let our fists rise skywards in a perpetual greeting between the rebels of this world and all those marching against it. But also let this happen for a "fare thee well" to the rebels who "departed" early, Lampros Foundas [a member of the Revolutionary Struggle], Mauricio Morales and to the long list of comrades who prematurely paid the price of armed struggle's difficult beauty. In this journey of fire amid the darkness we are not alone. We always have by our side our imprisoned brothers, captured in the hostilities with the opponent, who once again raised honor and dignity above the fear of prison. Therefore greetings to wish strength to the imprisoned comrades and to act as a reminder to the prison guards and prison wardens that no dignified prisoner is alone.

II) Militant anarchy, the new urban guerrilla movement

In recent years a situation has developed in Greece that makes any going back impossible. The radical anti-authoritarian trend stands out as the main expression of the internal enemy leaving Marxist rationales and left-wing reformism permanently consigned to the dustbin of history. Despite its contradictions, weaknesses and introspections, the anti-authoritarian internal enemy is present throughout the spectrum of rebellion: from posters and aggressive marches to sabotage, armed robberies, bomb attacks and political executions.

This is the climate of an era nurtured in fire within which the CCF organized itself and struck. After about three years of tenacious action with more than 200 arson and bomb attacks we continue to believe that our actions are just a drop in the ocean of the immensity of our desire for revolution. The Conspiracy derives from a new wave of revolutionary anarchy that has forcefully entered the field of conflict and social challenge dynamically. Through the targeting of our actions and the arguments of our proclamations we designate ourselves to be a part of the militant anarchy of the new urban guerrilla movement, which exercises incessant armed criticism to the tyranny of those "on the top" and the compromises of those "beneath".

The targets attacked, namely the car dealerships, banks, police stations, security companies, politician's offices, parliament, churches, courts, prisons, embassies ... for us they are just buildings which, despite how many kilograms of explosives we will place, will be rebuilt from scratch with more cameras, more security, seemingly increasingly impregnable. Meanwhile the ensuing mass media propaganda either conceals some attacks by covering them with a veil of silence or, where it is forced to publicize them (bombs, executions) depoliticizes them by slandering them. At the same time, employing assimilation of the matter, it "fits" them in between advertisements for the "new dish washing liquid" and the reality TV programs of virtual reality, turning them into a neutral product of an indifferent item of information. That is why our essential target is not merely locked doors, office walls and department store display windows, but rather it is blowing up and sabotaging the social relationships which make these symbols of authority acceptable....

III) The antisocial trend and society's complicity

Therefore we belong to the antisocial trend of anarchy, which not only opposes the state but society as well, because we perceive that the authority relies not only on force and the dictates of the state command posts, but also on compromise, the acceptance and resignation of a silent crowd, which has learned to cheer for national successes, celebrate for its sports team, change mood with the button on the remote control, fall in love with shop windows and false models, hate foreigners, look out for itself and close its eyes to the lack of real living This crowd of complacent citizens rises up from its couch only when the warmth of its petty ownership is threatened.

The economic crisis in Greece and its consequences, already constitute the new picture of social cannibalism. The social explosions of the majority of workers which erupt claim exclusively the financial demands of their own trade unions. In fact, frequently the labour protests (truck driver strikes, blockage of ports by dock workers and others) cause a social short circuit and discontent among the other workers. Of course this scene alternates and those who are currently on the streets "claiming their own", tomorrow will confront others who would be striking for their own claims (eg. lorry drivers against farmers' blockades, citizens against striking civil servants, parents against striking teachers, and others). All these social protests impoverish our language and our consciousness, claiming a better state, a better job, better education, better healthcare, but never daring to touch upon how the issue is not simply whether we are less or more poor than we were yesterday, but that we are living in a way that does not fulfil us. Our existence is humiliated by the commands of every boss, our wishes are reflected in the shop window dummy, our disobedience is imprisoned by the uniformed patrols, enjoyment becomes a product in the supermarkets' shiny shelves, expression loses its face behind face masks, communication becomes a key on the keyboard in front of cold computer screens. All these losses are worth something more than mere protests for a handful of euros. They deserve our wholehearted commitment to the new urban guerrilla movement.

The new urban guerrilla movement is the assertion of our existence, the alliance with the authentic aspect of life, the difficult and rough path in a society that has sold out any trace of conscience. Today everyone is looking out for himself, turning his disappointment into cynicism and indifference and the only thing that matters to him is how he will accommodate himself at any price. Authority plays game of "divide and rule" well because it has an easy opponent. When it faces a degenerate society engrossed more in the virtual reality of reality TV shows than in real life, then it takes no particular effort to divide it, because already it is divided between the interest-free installments of consumer joy and the new mortgage loans of petty-bourgeois illusions.

As for life? Life now is absent from this city, now there is only the noise of cars, the voices of everyday instructions and the pictures of ads shooting at us all day. That is why we believe that class consciousness is dead and buried beneath the foundations of modern civilization. Whoever today speaks of class war has the past in his mouth. We will elaborate lest we be misunderstood. Because it is obvious that we are not living in a glass jar of pure ideologies, we are aware that the essence of the system lies in producing social and economic inequalities. For the few rich to exist, many poor will have to exist. Therefore when we say that the class war is an outdated concept, we do not mean that there are no social classes, but rather that we believe that there is no class consciousness. So therefore if the oppressed and exploited of this world refuse to become aware of their position, to stand up and attack the palace of the "czars" who have taken away from us so much, we do not intend to play the role of popular awakening.

On the contrary, through our reasoning and our actions we wish to avoid the old trap of engaging in revolutionary thought, which persisted in approaching history against a black and white background, with the bad state and good oppressed. We reject the standardized reading tablets, the "eternal" truths and the easy conclusions. That is why there are no economic analyses in our texts. This does not mean that we do not recognize the crucial position the economy plays as the cornerstone of the system. However, how can we describe in economic terms the blank empty eyes of a child begging at traffic lights, the queues at the soup kitchens, the accounts which keep on accumulating and the cut-off electricity supply, the loans, the unpaid rents, but chiefly how to avoid becoming trapped in a humanitarian compassion without seeking to attribute the responsibility for the inaction of those who are subjected to the economy's whipping without reacting?

It is a fact that personally we are all experiencing oppression daily, but the difference lies in what each one of us does about it. Some pretend to ignore it and switch the remote control to another channel, some others blame the foreigners "who are taking our jobs", others ask for more policing, others become police officers and private security guards themselves, others continue to wear partisan blinkers, others are studying at university to get into the "fast" track or to feed their parents' illusions, others find hiding places to forget, such as conspicuous consumption at Ermou Street [main shopping street in Athens] and spending weekends at Gazi [a fashionable night spot in Athens] and a specific few give disillusion a voice and wear it as a hood, concocting new plans of overthrow within the modern crematoria of the metropolis.

Understanding by now has become bankrupt and explanations are seeking the reason. The economy is not simply a scientific methodology for interpreting the world, but primarily it is a social relationship which is becoming founded as a criterion distinguishing people. When in the decade of the 1990s authority could offer the promise of the world of plenty, the current voices of protest made way for consumerist smiles without regard to how such happiness is always built on the backs of the misery of other people (collapse of the eastern bloc, immigration, civil wars). Now it is the turn of western man to wrestle with the impasses of the culture he created. Standing against the overlooking of social responsibilities, we exercise our criticism practically, not only seeking to short-circuit the system economically but also [to short-circuit] the system itself and its citizens. That is why the Conspiracy does not speak the language of class analysis, but rather it engages in the deliberate choice of attacking, of armed struggle and of revolution for an overthrow of the entire structure.

We do not need a vision of massive social uprising to believe in and to anchor ourselves to something, because we respect ourselves and have faith in our comrades, and also because of our deep conviction that what we are living through is not life. That is why we have removed from our vocabulary the supposed revolutionary underlying subject of the oppressed proletariat…

APPENDIX 3

Attack communiqué by the Lambros Foundas Guerrilla Formation for the bomb attack against the Caravel Hotel in Athens, on 23 November 2010:

For a long time we have been following the path of denial and of urban guerilla warfare. This is the point where anger and hatred about the misery of daily life and destroyed human relations encounter conscience and determination. This is the point where actions give meaning to words ... In this case the actions are of a warlike nature ... They target the enemy, dismantle the system by dissolving the images and idols of a hypnotized society that has learned to kneel, to obey, to bow its head.

But rebels do not bow their heads ... there is too much blood, too much violence. Those who truly love justice have no right to invoke love. They stand upright ... with the head up and the eyes focused. What business can love have with these proud hearts? Love makes you slowly-slowly bow the head ... Our neck cannot be easily bowed.

With clenched fists raised in the air we welcome the captive members of the Revolutionary Organization Conspiracy of Cells of Fire, G. Tsakalos, P. Argyriou, Ch. Chatzimichelakis, and anarchist revolutionary G. Skouloudis, for their proud stance and declare that their stance makes us even more dangerous, even more aggressive.

Therefore, in our wish to deal yet another blow against the enemy's prestige, commandos from our formation, early in the morning of Tuesday, 23 November, placed a powerful incendiary device, similar to the one we placed at the HSBC Bank in the Psychiko area, at the side entrance of the DIVANI CARAVEL hotel, just a few meters away from the main entrance, behind the back of the security guards and the cop who was on sentry duty. At this point we want to stress that the small size of the device we used was chosen solely in order to avoid causing any deaths or injuries to those working [at the hotel]! This is despite our belief that for hotels like this one, where the local and foreign political and economic elite is staying, doing business, meeting and being entertained, the only thing they deserve is pillage and total destruction.

The aim of the attack was to spread terror among the hotel's residents, among them many deputies, to strike at the country's image and its heavy industry called tourism, and at the same time show that Athens was not, is not, and will not be a safe city, nor a fertile ground for "safe investments" with "a high yield". After all, the area where we acted is an area with increased surveillance and controls, since within a few hundred meters is the location of the YMET [Unit for Enforcing Public Order] headquarters, the Kaisariani Traffic Department, the Kaissariani and Pangrati police precincts, as well as the Hilton Hotel, which on the particular evening our operation was carried out was under the "watchful" eye of the MAT [Police Riot Units], in view of the press conference the troika was due to give the next morning.

The enemy is not invulnerable, in fact this has been demonstrated by the nights of fire offered to us by the rebel formations in Athens and Thessaloniki who, with the quality of their attacks and their words, excite us and make us impatient for the next hits.

Comrades, we are organizing the rebellion, we are conspiring, we are attacking, we leave no room for the enemy, we are beside him, we are monitoring his movements, we go uninvited to homes, to hotels, to luxury shops and we always escape, leaving the fire burning behind us

Our own day will come … and when it does come, you will be looking for holes to hide, you bastards …

NOTES

1. INTRODUCTION

1. Xiros's information led also to the discovery of the group's main arsenal in three flats in central Athens. The flats—one of them rented by Xiros himself—contained a number of the sixty anti-tank rockets stolen by 17N from an army base in northern Greece in 1989, the typewriter used to produce the group's early communiqués, 17N's red flag with the trademark five-pointed star as well as grenades, wigs, communiqués and posters of Che Guevara, Karl Marx and Aris Velouhiotis, a Greek Second World War resistance fighter. One of the weapons, a G-3 rifle, was used to kill the group's last victim, the British defence attaché in Athens, Stephen Saunders, who was shot dead in June 2000 as he drove to work.
2. Giotopoulos, whose fingerprints were identified by Greek police in 17N's two Athens hideaways containing the group's arsenal, maintained throughout the trial that he had no involvement whatsoever with 17N. In denying all 963 charges against him, Giotopoulos asserted that 'the role of the [17N] leader was a police fabrication' and that the main reason why he was put behind bars was because 'the Americans, the British and their collaborators in the Greek government wanted it like that'. According to Giotopoulos, the charges were nothing more than 'a cheap construct of the Americans and British signed by prosecutors and former provincial police and based on confessions taken in a hospital intensive care unit from people destroyed by psychotropic drugs and blackmail', referring to Savvas Xiros's hospital confession soon after the June 2002 botched bomb attack. Giotopoulos also denied that handwritten corrections on drafts of 17N proclamations were his own as the state prosecutor charged, and claimed that his fingerprints, found in 17N safe houses, including a left thumbprint on a mobile phone manual, were transferred by agents onto movable objects. Giotopoulos was convicted as 'the clear mastermind and leader' of 17N. The prosecutor characterised him as 'the root of evil both before and after his arrest' and proposed for him a sentence that amounted to 2,412 years, which is what Giotopoulos eventually received. Giotopoulos's defence team maintained throughout that physical evidence was scant and that his conviction was basically the product of testimonies by other accused 17N

members, a violation of the Greek criminal code's provision, which specifically states that the testimony of a guilty person alone cannot be sufficient in establishing guilt. Son of a prominent Trotskyite theoretician and activist of the pre-Second World War era, Giotopoulos studied in France during the years of the Colonels' junta, where in 1969 he helped to found the radical May 29 movement, which advocated armed rebellion against the Greek military regime. In 1971 he was found guilty in absentia by the Greek authorities of creating an armed organisation and was sentenced to five years in jail. He remained in Paris where he founded a new group, the Popular Armed Struggle (LEA), which from its inception was divided over how to direct its energies. Giotopoulos was in favour of aggressive acts of urban guerrilla warfare and split from the group with a small clique of others. Returning to Athens after the fall of the Colonels' regime in 1975, he came, according to Greek police files, into contact with members of Greece's other prominent urban guerrilla group, Revolutionary Popular Struggle (ELA), and attempted unsuccessfully to persuade them to sign on to a plan to abduct CIA station chief Richard Welch. Welch was eventually shot dead outside his home on 23 December, 1975 by 17N.

3. Other life sentences in addition to twenty-five years, the maximum sentence under Greek law, were handed down to Savvas Xiros (six life terms) his brother Christodoulos (ten life terms), Vassilis Tzortzatos (four life terms) and Iraklis Kostaris (four life terms). Five other members (Vassilis, the younger of the Xiros brothers, Costas Karatsolis, Patroklos Tselentis, Sotyris Kondylis and Costas Telios) received the maximum twenty-five-year sentence. Telios, who had handed himself in and was diagnosed with severe psychiatric disability, was the only convicted member to receive a suspended sentence and walk free pending an appellate trial, on the condition that he reported to his local police precinct monthly and did not leave the country. Only four convicts received less than the maximum twenty-five years: Thomas Serifis (seventeen years), Dionysis Georgiadis (nine years) and eight years each to Nikos Papanastasiou and Pavlos Serifis.
4. See '17N: I Diki den Edose apandisseis' [17N: The Trial Failed to Provide Answers] in *Kathimerini tis Kyriakis*, 30 December 2003.
5. See for example, Alison Jamieson, 'Identity and Morality in the Italian Red Brigades', in *Terrorism and Political Violence*, Vol. 2, No. 4 (Winter 1990), pp. 508–20; Alberto Franceschini, *Mara Renato e Io, Storia dei fondatori delle BR* (Milano: Armando Mondatori Editore, 1988).
6. As US State Department intelligence threat analyst Dennis Pluchinsky put it to the author, 'I have never seen a terrorist group unravel so quickly.' Back in the early 1990s, Pluchinsky had prophetically written that 'the Achilles heel for 17N may be the absence of any known supporter or sympathizer base. In essence, unlike the RAF and DEV SOL, 17N has not demonstrated an ability to reorganize after police arrests. The group may be susceptible to a police "knockout punch"—like AD and the CCC. 17N appears to be small, possibly single cell, self-sufficient group that could become demoralized and unravelled with the arrests of one or

two of its members.' See *Europe's Red Terrorists: The Fighting Communist Organizations* (London: Frank Cass, 1992), p. 48.

7. See, for example, Audrey Kurth Cronin, *How Terrorism Ends: Understanding the Decline and Demise of Terrorist Campaign*, (Princeton, NJ: Princeton University Press, 2009); for specific case studies see Rogelio Alonso, 'Why Do Terrorists Stop? Analyzing Why ETA Members Abandon or Continue with Terrorism' in *Studies in Conflict & Terrorism* (Vol. 34, No 9, 2011) pp. 696–716; Peter Waldmann, 'How Terrorism Ceases: The Tupamaros in Uruguay' in *Studies in Conflict & Terrorism* (Vol. 34, No 9, 2011) pp. 717–731; Assaf Moghadan 'Failure and Disengagement in Red Army Faction' in *Studies in Conflict & Terrorism* (Vol. 35, No. 2, 2012) pp. 156–181.
8. The tried-and-tested formula of the Koufodinas legal team with regards to media interviews is, as was explained to me by one Greek journalist who has been granted 'an interview' as follows: 'you send his lawyer Ioanna Kourtovik a list of questions which she will then go through, eliminate the ones that she's not happy with and then pass them on to Koufodinas. Once you get Koufodinas's answers back, you publish them exactly as they are. Any slight change, stylistic or otherwise, on publication and you and your newspaper are blacklisted or sued.' Author interview with journalist, Athens, 11 September 2010.
9. There were also times when asking predetermined questions became difficult as other issues that seemed pertinent and important to the person being interviewed were brought up such as the person's medical condition at the time or his interpersonal relations with other prisoners.
10. It is a risk to try to penetrate the mental processes of a 17N terrorist with involvement in eighty-five terrorist acts in the space of seventeen years but Xiros seems unable after all these years to reconcile himself to his own failures, and is sensitive to the charge that he informed on his comrades. In a hard-fought but pointless battle in rebuilding his 17N terrorist image Xiros wrote a memoir drawing on his Evagellismos Hospital experiences, entitled in Greek *I Mera Ekeini: 1560 Ores stin Entatiki. Mia Martyria gia to diko mas Guantanamo* [On That Day: 1560 Hours in Intensive Care: An Eyewitness Account of our Guantanamo] and published in 2006 by his Spanish partner Alicia Romero. 'It is an account', Xiros writes in the introduction, 'of the Mengelian interrogations which aimed at the depths of existence, that with insidious means disturb, invalidating critical judgement, that with profane methods strike to bend the will, to bind it, drag it along to paths it would never have willingly traveled.' By 'Mengelian' Xiros refers to Josef Rudolf Mengele, also known as 'the Angel of Death', a German SS officer and a physician in the Nazi concentration camp Auschwitz. Mengele gained notoriety for being one of the SS physicians who supervised the selection of arriving transports of prisoners, determining who was to be killed and who was to become a forced laborer, but is far more infamous for performing human experiments on camp inmates.
11. Interview with Marinos Pittaridis, Athens, 19 May 2006.

2. GREEK POLITICAL VIOLENCE IN CONTEXT

1. See Minas Samatas, 'Greek McCarthyism: A Comparative Assessment of Greek Post-Civil War Repressive Anticommunism and the US Truman-McCarthy Era' in *Journal of the Hellenic Diaspora*, Vol. 13, Nos. 3–4 (Fall-Winter 1986), p. 15.
2. Constantine Tsoucalas, *The Greek Tragedy* (Harmondsworth: Penguin, 1969), p. 115.
3. Samatas, 'Greek McCarthyism', p. 35.
4. See David H. Close, 'The Legacy' in David H. Close (ed.), *The Greek Civil War, 1943–1950: Studies in Polarization*, (London: Routledge, 1993), pp. 218–220.
5. Tsoucalas, *The Greek Tragedy*, p. 118.
6. P. Nikiforos Diamandouros, 'Regime Change and the Prospects for Democracy in Greece: 1974–1983' in Guillermo O'Donnell, Philippe C. Schmitter and Laurence Whitehead (eds), *Transitions from Authoritarian Rule: Prospects for Democracy* (Baltimore: Johns Hopkins University Press, 1986), pp. 140–42.
7. Mario S. Modiano, 'Greek Political Troubles', in *The World Today*, Vol. 21, No. 1 (January 1965), pp. 35–40.
8. Nicos P. Mouzelis, *Modern Greece: Facets of Underdevelopment* (London: Macmillan, 1978), p. 133.
9. 'We have long been witnessing', Kollias, the junta's new premier, said in his statement on the day of the coup, 'a crime committed against our people and our nation. Unscrupulous and base party compromises, shameful recklessness of a great part of the press, methodical attacks on undermining all institutions, complete debasement of parliament, all-round slander, paralysis of the state machinery, complete lack of understanding of the burning problems of our youth, moral decline, secret and open collaboration with subversion, and finally, constant inflammatory slogans of unscrupulous demagogues, have destroyed the country's peace, created an atmosphere of anarchy and chaos, hatred and discord, and led us to the brink of national catastrophe' cited from Keith R. Legg, *Politics in Modern Greece*, (Stanford: Stanford University Press, 1969), p. 227.
10. See Richard Clogg, 'The Ideology of the Revolution of 21 April 1967', in Richard Clogg and George Yannopoulos (eds), *Greece Under Military Rule*, (London: Secker & Warburg, 1972), p. 36.
11. See Thanos Veremis, *The Military in Greek Politics: From Independence to Democracy* (London: Hurst, 1997), pp. ix-x.
12. Nancy Bermeo, 'Classification and Consolidation: Some Lessons from the Greek Dictatorship', in *Political Science Quarterly*, Vol. 110, No. 3 (1995), pp. 449–50.
13. Panayote E. Dimitras, 'Changes in Public Attitudes', in Kevin Featherstone & Dimitrios Katsoudas (eds), *Political Change in Greece: Before and After the Colonels* (London: Croom Helm, 1987), p. 78; see *the Economist*, Survey: Greece, 31 July 1971.
14. Angelos Elephantis, *Ston Asterismo tou Laikismou* [In the Constellation of Populism] (Athens: O Politis, 1991), pp. 77–83.

15. The end of the dictatorship, it must be emphasized, and the surrender of power to a civilian government, was neither the result of a military counter-coup in Athens nor of a popular upheaval from below. Rather, it resulted from the 20 July Turkish invasion of northern Cyprus and the inability of the Colonels to handle the crisis and deal with a rapidly deteriorating situation. When a general mobilization collapsed in chaos, revealing that the politicization of the armed forces over the previous seven years had compromised their ability to defend the country's territorial integrity, the chiefs of staff, with the acquiescence of the military President of the Republic, General P. Gizikis, decided to call in the politicians. In less than twenty-four hours, Konstantinos Karamanlis returned from his French exile to rescue Greece from the brink of war with Turkey and to preside over the transition to a civilian rule.
16. Raymond Carr, *Modern Spain 1875–1980* (Oxford: Oxford University Press, 1980), p. 106.
17. See Alkis Rigos, 'Foititiko Kinima kai Diktatoria' [The Student Movement and the Military Dictatorship], *Anti* (No. 344, 1987), pp. 54–55.
18. See *Vassika Politika Keimena, 1970–1974* [Essential Political Texts, 1970–1974], (Athens: Epanastatiko Kommounistiko Kinima Elladas (EKKE), 1974), pp. 46–47; see also EKKE in 'The left of the left', *Eleftherotypia*, 18 June 1976.
19. Stelios Kouloglou and Yiannis Floros, 'I Katalipsi tis Nomikis—Proagellos tou Polytechniou' [The Occupation of the Athens Law School—Prelude to the Polytechnic], *Anti* No. 199, (1982), pp. 23–25.
20. Stavros Lygeros, *Foititiko Kinima kai Taxiki Pali stin Ellada, Tomos 1* [The Student Movement and Class Struggle in Greece, Vol. 1] (Athens: Ekdotiki Omada Ergassia, 1977), pp. 193–201, 204–209.
21. Antonis Davanelos, *Noemvris 1973: I exegerssi* [November 1973: The Revolt] (Athens: Ekdosseis Ergatiki Dimikratia, 2nd ed. 1995), p. 4.
22. See Georgia K. Polydorides, 'Equality of Opportunity in the Greek Higher Education System: The Impact of Reform Policies' and Maria Eliou, 'Those Whom Reform Forgot', both in Andreas M. Kazamias (ed.), 'Symposium on Educational Reform in Greece', *Comparative Education Review* Vol. 22, No. 1 (February 1978), pp. 80–81 and p. 67.
23. Henry Wasser, 'A Survey of Recent Trends in Greek Higher Education', *Journal of the Hellenic Diaspora*, Vol. 6, No. 1 (1979), p. 85.
24. See George Psacharopoulos and Andreas M. Kazamias, 'Student Activism in Greece: A Historical and Empirical Analysis' in *Higher Education*, No. 9 (1980), p. 130.
25. See Dionyssis Karageorgas, 'Oi Oikonomikes Synepeies tis Stratiotikis Diktatorias' [The Economic Consequences of the Military Dictatorship], *Anti*, No. 1 (1974), pp. 41–46.
26. See Tariq Ali and Susan Watkins, *1968: Marching in the Streets* (London: Bloomsbury, 1998), p. 57.
27. Loukas Axelos, 'Publishing Activity and the Movement of Ideas in Greece',

Journal of the Hellenic Diaspora Vol. 11, No. 2 (Summer 1984), p. 13; See also Petros Efthymiou, 'O Apoichos stin Ellada' [The After-effects of May '68 on Greece] in 'May '68: Thirty Years After', *To Vima*, Special supplement, 10 May 1998.

28. Dimitris Haralambis, *Stratos kai Politiki Exoussia: I domi tis exoussias stin metemfyliaki Ellada* [Political Power and The Military: The Power Structure in Post-Civil War Greece] (Athens: Exandas, 1985), pp. 296–302.
29. Axelos, 'Publishing Activity', p. 21.
30. Ibid., p. 23.
31. Wasser, 'A Survey of Recent Trends', p. 86.
32. Ibid.
33. Ibid., p. 87.
34. See 'Anakoinossi tis Antifassistikis Antiimberialistikis Spoudastikis Parataxis Elladas' (AASPE) [Announcement of the Antifascist Anti-imperialist Student Front of Greece (AASPE)], dated 27 November 1973; see also 'Anakoinossi tou Epanastatikou Kommounistikou Kinimatos Elladas (EKKE) kai tis Antifassistikis Antiimberialistikis Spoudastikis Parataxis Elladas' (AASPE) [Announcement of the Revolutionary Communist Movement of Greece (EKKE) and the Antifascist Antiimperialist Student Front (AASPE)], dated 31 December 1973.
35. See 'Polytechneio: Pera apo ton Mytho' [Polytechnic: Beyond the Myth], *Anti*, No. 6 (1974), pp. 14–16 and 24.
36. The Kinima 20is Oktomvri [The 20th October Movement] was formed in 1969 from ex-EDA members with cells both in Greece and abroad.
37. See for example, 'To Polytechneio mesa apo ta keimena tou' [The Polytechnic through its texts], *Dekapenthimeros Politis*, No. 2 (19 November, 1983), p. 32.
38. See Lygeros, *Foititiko Kinima, T. 1*, pp. 86–98.
39. Olympios Dafermos, *To antidiktatoriko foititiko kinima 1972–1973* [The Anti-Dictatorial Student Movement, 1972–1973] (Athens: Themelio, 1992), p. 124.
40. Ibid.
41. See *Eleftherotypia* special on the November 1973 events, 15–16 November, 1976.
42. Yiorgos Votsis, *Se Mavro Fondo* [Against the Dark Background] (Athens: Stochastis, 1984), pp. 241–245.
43. According to the *Eleftherotypia* of 29 July 1975, the majority of the 100,000 junta sympathisers removed from their posts only a mere 200 were appointees and collaborators of the military with important positions in the state apparatus.
44. See, for instance, *Kokkini Simaia* [Red Flag] No. 1 (October 1974) and Nos.2–3 (November-December 1974); see also Political announcements by Epanastatiko Kommounistiko Kinima Elladas (EKKE), dated 1, 28 March; 8, 21 April; and 16 May 1975.
45. Epanastatiko Kommounistiko Kinima Elladas (EKKE) [Revolutionary Communist Movement of Greece]; Organossi Marxiston Leniniston Elladas (OMLE) [Marxist-Leninist Organization of Greece]; Marxistiko Leninistiko Kommounistiko Komma Elladas (ML/KKE)[Marxist-Leninist Party of Greece (ML/

KKE)]; Rixi yia mia Proleratiaki Aristera (RIXI) [Rupture for a Proletarian Left]; Laiki Metopiki Protovoulia (LMP) [Popular Front Initiative]; Kommounistiki Organossi Machitis (KO. MACHITIS) [Communist Organization Machitis]; Synepis Aristeri Kinissi Elladas (SAKE) [Reliable Marxist-Leninist Movement]; Kinissi Ellinon Marxiston Leniniston (KEML) [Marxist-Leninist Movement]; and Organossi Kommouniston Marxiston-Leniniston Elladas (OKMLE) [Communist Organization of Marxist-Leninist of Greece].

46. Ergatiki Diethnistiki Enossi (EDE) [Workers' Internationalist Union]; Organossi Kommouniston Diethniston Elladas (OKDE) [Communist Organization of Greek Internationalists]; Kommounistiki Diethnistiki Enossi (KDE) [Communist Internationalist Union]; Organossi Sosialistiki Epanastassi (OSE) Organization Socialist Revolution]; Epanastatiko Kommunistiko Komma (EKK) [Revolutionary Communist Party]; and Sosialistiki Organossi Ergazomenon (SOE) [Socialist Organization of Workers].
47. See 17N attack communiqué against US Navy Capt. George Tsantes and his Greek driver Nikolaos Veloutsos, dated October 1983.
48. ELA manifesto: 'Yia tin anaptyxi tou Ellinikou Laikou kai Epanastatikou Kinimatos' [For the development of the Greek Popular and Revolutionary Movement], dated June/July 1978, p. 16.
49. Ibid.
50. Ibid.
51. The group appeared for the first time on 23 December 1975, when three unmasked men stalked Richard Welch, the CIA's station chief in Athens, shooting him down at point-blank range in front of his wife and Greek driver. By choosing such a high-profile target, 17N aimed to put itself immediately on the map and establish credibility as a revolutionary group. However, this strategy produced the reverse effect. Because the operation was conducted with high precision and efficiency, the Greek security services dismissed the responsibility claims of a previously unknown organization calling itself Revolutionary Organization 17 November as the work of cranks. Police officials believed at the time that both extreme left and right were trying to embarrass each other by sending fraudulent communiqués to the media. Without solid leads and given the vicious atmosphere of the period, the police resorted to imposing a ban on publicizing reports in the press forty-eight hours after the assassination, which only served to exacerbate media speculation.

3. GUERRILLA LEADER: DIMITRIS KOUFODINAS AND THE REVOLUTIONARY ORGANIZATION 17 NOVEMBER (17N)

1. For a detailed analysis of 17N's historical antecedents, ideology, strategy and attacks see George Kassimeris, *Europe's Last Red Terrorists: The Revolutionary Organization 17 November* (London: Hurst, 2001).
2. On the way the Greek media reacted to the Koufodinas unexpected surrender see

Kathimerini and *Ta Nea*, 6 September 2002 and *Kyriakatiki Eleftherotypia* and *To Vima tis Kyriakis*, 8 September 2002. See also 'Deka apantisseis gia to grifo Koufodina,' [Ten answers for the Koufodinas puzzle] *Eleftherotypia*, 12 September 2002, and 'Greece's most wanted surrenders', *The Guardian*, 6 September 2002.

3. Nikos Giannopoulos in his court testimony, Korydallos prison chambers, 25 July 2003.
4. *Metro* magazine journalist Nikos Vafeiadis in his court testimony, Korydallos prison chambers, 26 July 2003.
5. Cited in *Eleftherotypia*, 9 September 2002.
6. Judd was attacked by two men on a motorcycle at a traffic stop as he was driving a shipment of diplomatic mail to the US Air Force base at Athens Hellenicon airport. The attackers pulled alongside Judd's car and it was Koufodinas, according to the charge sheet, who fired five rounds against him with 17N's .45-calibre signature weapon. Judd, instinctively, accelerated, jumped over the median strip and sped away.
7. Koufodinas's opening remarks before the court. The nine-month trial—the longest in modern Greek history—was held in a purpose-built courtroom in Athens's largest maximum-security prison where a three-member tribunal convicted fifteen members of the group, while another four defendants were acquitted for lack of sufficient evidence.
8. Bruce Hoffman, *Inside Terrorism* (London: Victor Gollancz, 1998).
9. See 'O antrhropos pou pire tin efthini' [The man who took responsibility], *Kyriakatiki Eleftherotypia*, 30 November 2003 and 'Esosse tin…timi tous' [He saved…their honour] in *Ta Nea*, 8 December 2003.
10. Court proceedings, Korydallos prison court chambers, 23 July 2003.
11. 'He had the look of a man who knew something damaging about every one of his co-defendants', a Greek political commentator who was also covering the opening of the 17N trial said to the author.
12. Court proceedings, Korydallos prison chambers, 24 July 2003.
13. Letter to *Eleftherotypia* newspaper, 10 September 2002.
14. Court proceedings, Korydallos prison chambers, 24 July 2003.
15. Ibid.
16. On 17N's tactics, targets and operational evolution between 1975 to 1980 see George Kassimeris, *Europe's Last Red Terrorists*, pp. 72–5.
17. Court proceedings, Korydallos prison chambers, 24 July 2003.
18. Ibid.
19. Ibid.
20. Ibid.
21. Ibid.
22. Ibid.
23. Ibid.
24. Ibid.

25. Ibid.
26. Ibid.
27. 'We have but one answer to all these reports', said the eight-page communiqué sent to the *Eleftherotypia* newspaper. 'Come and get us, if you can'. See *Eleftherotypia*, 16 March 1999 and *Athens News*, 17 March 1999.
28. Court proceedings, Korydallos prison chambers, 24 July 2003.
29. Ibid.
30. Ibid.
31. Ibid.
32. Ibid.
33. Ibid.
34. Ibid.
35. Ibid.
36. Ibid.
37. Ibid.
38. Ibid.
39. Ibid.
40. In the 17N's 'Manifesto 1992', the communiqué writer acknowledges that it would have never been able to survive and avoid capture, had the group not drawn lessons from the Red Brigades experience. See 'Manifesto 1992', dated 17 November 1992.
41. David Moss, 'Analyzing Italian Political Violence as a Sequence of Communicative Acts: The Red Brigades, 1970–1982', *Social Analysis*, No. 3 (May 1983), p. 85.
42. Court proceedings, Korydallos prison chambers, 24 July 2003.
43. Ibid.
44. Ibid.
45. Ibid.
46. Ibid.
47. Ibid.
48. Ibid.
49. Ibid.
50. See Garrett O'Boyle, 'Theories of Justification and Political Violence: Examples from Four Groups', *Terrorism and Political Violence*, Vol. 14, No. 2 (Summer 2002), p. 30.
51. Court proceedings, Korydallos prison chambers, 24 July 2003.
52. Ibid.
53. Ibid.
54. Ibid.
55. Ibid.
56. Ibid.
57. Ibid.
58. Ibid.
59. See Koufodinas interview in *Eleftherotypia* newspaper, 7 December 2002.

60. Koufodinas's defence lawyer, Ioanna Kourtovik, acts as his spokesperson and representative. A strong-minded professional woman and activist, Kourtovik made clear to me over a meeting in her office in Athens that any interview with Koufodinas would only take place on the condition that she had right of approval of the final copy. Because Kourtovik, a campaigning lawyer, has made a name representing political activists and militants she has been labelled by some sections of the Greek media as a 'sympathizer'. See an article she wrote during 17N's trial in *Eleftherotypia*, 29 December 2002.
61. See Aggeliki Sotiropoulou interview in *Ta Nea*, 19 April 2004.
62. Koufodinas interview in *Eleftherotypia*, 7 December 2002.
63. Ibid.
64. Ibid.
65. Ibid.
66. Court proceedings, Korydallos prison chambers, 24 July 2003.
67. For a operational and ideological profile of RS see Chapter 6.
68. Interview with *Proto Thema* tabloid newspaper, 13 July 2007; the Sect of Revolutionaries group first became known in February 2009 with a shooting at the headquarters of Alter TV which caused no injuries. In June 2009, the group killed an anti-terrorist police officer and in July 2010 an investigative journalist, Sokratis Giolias. Giolias was shot dead outside his Athens home on 19 July, in front of his pregnant wife. The group promised to step up attacks on police, businessmen, prison guards and the 'corrupt' media—and, for the first time, threatened holidaymakers. 'Tourists should learn that Greece is no longer a safe haven of capitalism', its declaration said. 'We intend to turn it into a war zone of revolutionary activity with arson, sabotage, violent demonstrations, bombings and assassinations, and not a country that is a destination for holidays and pleasure.' In an accompanying picture, the group displayed an arsenal that included AK-47 assault rifles, semi-automatic pistols and brass knuckledusters. The group, which launched no further attacks, ended its communiqué with a threat: 'Our guns are full and they are ready to speak', it said. 'We are at war with your democracy.'
69. Ibid.
70. Ibid.
71. Ibid.
72. *Memorias del Calabozo* was published in Spanish in December 2000. The Greek edition, translated by Koufodinas, was brought out in 2009 by Koukida publishers as *Imerologio Filakis*.
73. The Tupamaros, also known as the MLN-T (Movimiento de Liberación Nacional-Tupamaros or Tupamaros National Liberation Movement) were created in the early 1960s by Raúl Sendic, a Marxist lawyer and activist who had sought to bring about social change peacefully by unionizing sugarcane workers. When the workers were continually repressed, Sendic knew that he would never meet his goals peacefully. On 5 May 1962 Sendic, along with a handful of sugarcane

workers, attacked and burned the Uruguayan Union Confederation building in Montevideo. The lone casualty was Dora Isabel López de Oricchio, a nursing student who was in the wrong place at the wrong time. According to many, this was the first action of the Tupamaros. The Tupamaros themselves, however, point to the 1963 attack on the Swiss Gun Club, which netted them several weapons, as their first act. In the early 1960s the Tupamaros committed a series of low-level crimes such as robberies, often distributing part of the money to Uruguay's poor. The name Tupamaro is derived from Túpac Amaru, last of the ruling members of the royal Inca line, who was executed by the Spanish in 1572. It was first associated with the group in 1964.

74. Koufodinas translation of *Memorias del Calabozo*, p. 13.
75. Ibid., p. 12.
76. Ibid.
77. Court proceedings, Korydallos prison chambers, 1 April 2003.
78. Peter Paret, 'Clausewitz' in P. Paret (ed.), *Makers of Modern Strategy* (Oxford: Oxford University Press, 1986), p. 200.
79. Court proceedings, Korydallos prison chambers, 24 July 2003.
80. Ibid.

4. EXIT 17N: PATROKLOS TSELENTIS AND SOTIRIS KONDYLIS

1. See Bruce Hoffman, *Inside Terrorism* (New York: Columbia University Press, 2006); Mark Sageman, *Understanding Terror Networks* (Philadelphia: University of Pennsylvania Press, 2004).
2. See Alison Jamieson, 'Entry, Discipline and Exit in the Italian Red Brigades' in *Terrorism and Political Violence* (Vol. 2 No. 1, 1990), pp. 1–20.
3. See John Horgan, *Walking Away from Terrorism* (London: Routledge, 2009).
4. See Joshua Geltzer, *US Counter-Terrorism Strategy and al-Qaeda* (London: Routledge, 2010); see also Daniel Byman, *The Five Front War: The Better Way to Fight Global Jihad* (London: Wiley, 2008).
5. The charges against Tselentis included participating in a criminal organization, construction, supply and possession of explosives, being an accomplice in grand weapons possession, repeated counts of attempted manslaughter, robbery that resulted in death and causing an explosion. These included the robbery of a National Bank branch in Petralona and the murder of police officer Christos Matis on 24 December 1984; the murder of *Apogevmatini* newspaper publisher Nikos Momferatos and his driver Panagiotis Rousetis on 21 February 1985 in Kolonaki; the murder of industrialist Dimitris Angelopoulos on 8 April 1986 in Kolonaki; the attempted murder of medical doctor Zaharias Kapsalakis on 4 February 1987; setting off a bomb in an air force bus carrying United States army officers in Rendi on 24 April 1987 in which thirteen people were injured; the attempted murder of US national George Carros on 21 January 1988 in Filothei, the murder through a booby-trapped car of US military attaché William Nordeen on 28 June 1988 in

Kefalari; and the raid on a police station in Vyrona in which weapons were stolen.

6. See David Moss, 'The Gift of Repentance: A Maussian Perspective on Twenty Years of Pentimento in Italy' in *European Journal of Sociology* (Vol. 42, No. 2, 2001) pp. 298–301.
7. Ted Robert Gurr, *Why Men Rebel* (Princeton, NJ: Princeton University Press, 1970), p. 195.
8. Ibid.
9. Ibid.
10. Ibid.
11. Ibid.
12. Ibid.
13. See Alison Jamieson, 'Identity and Morality in the Italian Red Brigades' in *Terrorism and Political Violence* (Vol. 2 No. 4, 1990), p. 513.
14. According to Marighella, this 'form of revolutionary armed struggle inevitably resembles certain forms of banditry, but the fundamental difference between the two is that revolutionaries do not expropriate from workers and ordinary people, do not violate their interests or harm them or their property. Revolutionaries do not attack the people, but combat dictatorship, the dominant classes and imperialism, and by doing so win the sympathy of the population. By making expropriations seem the work of bandits and by avoiding identifying themselves and their origins, the Brazilian revolutionaries managed to gain time by keeping the authorities in a state of uncertainty, preventing them from following specific trials.' Reproduced in Vicenzo Tessandori, *BR Imputazione: banda armata; Cronaca e documenti delle Brigate Rosse* (Milan: Garzanti, 1977), p. 24. It is worth mentioning that unlike the Red Brigades, which refrained from publicly claiming responsibility for bank 'expropriation' until 1975, 17N's long list of self-financing operations came known only after the group's arrests.
15. Tselentis court testimony, August 2003.
16. Ibid.
17. The occupation of the Athens Polytechnic in November 1973 provoked a major crisis to the apparatus as it became the epicentre of student dissent and served as an effective focus of opposition to the regime. Lasting for a mere three days (14–17 November) the revolt not only challenged the military regime but catalyzed popular mobilization in many sectors of Greek society. What had begun as a student protest against an authoritarian educational system escalated rapidly into a general political uprising against the military dictatorship.
18. Tselentis court testimony, August 2003.
19. Ibid.
20. Ibid.
21. 17N communiqué taking credit for the attack on Momferatos and his driver, undated.
22. Tselentis court testimony, August 2003

23. Ibid.
24. Ibid.
25. Ibid. See also Eamon Collins, *Killing Rage*, (London: Granta, 1997), p. 23–24.
26. Ibid.
27. Ibid.
28. Tselentis Korydallos court testimony, 5 July 2003.
29. Ibid.
30. Ibid.
31. Ibid.
32. Ibid.
33. Ibid.
34. Ibid.
35. Ibid.
36. Ibid.
37. Taken from an interview that was carried out by the anarcho-punk webzine Future Noir in 2002 (http://futurenoir.propagande.org).
38. Tselentis court testimony, 5 July 2003.
39. Tselentis court testimony, 5 July 2003.
40. Jamieson, p. 197.
41. Tselentis court testimony, 5 July 2003.
42. Ibid.
43. Ibid.
44. See Robert Meade, *Red Brigades: The Story of Italian Terrorism* (Basingstoke: Macmillan, 1990), p. 241.
45. Koufodinas court testimony, July 2003.
46. Author interview with T. Papagiannis, Athens, September 2006.
47. Kondylis court testimony, 28 August 2003.
48. Ibid.
49. Ibid.
50. Ibid.
51. Ibid.
52. Ibid.
53. Ibid.
54. Kondylis court testimony, 29 August 2003.
55. Kondylis court testimony, 28 August 2003.
56. Ibid.
57. Ibid.
58. Ibid.
59. Ibid.
60. Author interview, Athens, October 2010.
61. Alison Jamieson, *The Heart Attacked* (London: Marion Boyars, 1990), p. 234.
62. The words of a Front Linea pentito cited in Donatella Della Porta, *Social Movements, Political Violence, and the State: A Comparative Analysis of Italy and Germany*, (Cambridge: Cambridge University Press, 1995), p. 147.

63. Primo Moroni (ed.) *Le Parole la Lotta Armata* (Milano: Shake Edizioni, 1999), p. 31.
64. Donatella Della Porta, 'Leaving Underground Organizations: A Sociological Analysis of the Italian Case' in Tore Bjiorgo and John Horgan (eds) *Leaving Terrorism Behind: Individual and Collective Disengagement* (London: Routledge, 2009), p. 72.
65. Kondylis court testimony 29 August 2003.
66. Ibid.

5. ETERNAL REVOLUTIONARY: CHRISTOS TSIGARIDAS AND THE REVOLUTIONARY POPULAR STRUGGLE (ELA)

1. On organizational and operational differences between 17N and ELA see George Kassimeris, *Europe's Last Red Terrorists: The Revolutionary Organization 17 November* (London: Hurst, 2001). See also George Kassimeris, 'Greece: Twenty Years of Political Violence' in *Terrorism and Political Violence*, Vol. 7, No. 2 (Winter 1995), pp. 74–92.
2. Based on a number of off-the-record talks the author had with extra-parliamentary left activists active in the 1980s the consensus is that Tsigaridas had a much more significant role than he let the court believe.
3. Tsigaridas and the other four suspected ELA members (former mayor of Kimolos Angeletos Kannas, civil engineer Costas Agapiou, travel agent Irini Athanassaki and civil servant Michalis Kassimis) had been arrested in early 2003 and were originally sentenced to twenty-five years imprisonment each—the maximum possible—for involvement in ELA attacks. The court had originally sentenced the three men and a woman to 1,174 years each, but later revised the jail terms. The judge said they had played a secondary role in forty-two bombings and forty-eight murder attempts since 1983 by ELA, or People's Revolutionary Struggle. Angeletos Kanas, fifty-two, Costas Agapiou, fifty-six, Irene Athanasaki, fifty, and Christos Tsigaridas, sixty-four, were convicted by the special anti-terrorism court on just over half the charges they faced. They were not convicted of the more serious charges of actually orchestrating or carrying out any of the attacks, in which one policeman died, due to lack of evidence. The statute of limitations prevented them from being charged in connection with attacks more than twenty years old. They also escaped sentences under Greece's anti-terrorism legislation because the court found that ELA suspended operations in 1995—six years before the law came into force. In December 2009, an Athens appeal court overturned the original verdict, clearing them of involvement in a string of attacks, including a blast that killed a policeman in 1994, as it deemed that there was insufficient evidence to implicate them. Tsigaridas had already been released in January 2005 on grounds of ill health.
4. The Greek victory over the initial Italian offensive of October 1940 was the first Allied land victory of the Second World War, and helped raise morale in occupied Europe. Some historians, such as John Keegan, argue that it may have influenced

the course of the entire war by forcing Germany to postpone the invasion of the Soviet Union in order to assist Italy against Greece. This led to a delayed attack and subjected the German forces to the conditions of the harsh Russian winter, leading to their defeat at the Battle of Moscow.

5. On EAM/ELAS see Mark Mazower, *Inside Hitler's Greece: The Experience of Occupation 1941–44* (New Haven: Yale University Press, 1995).
6. Through special paraconstitutional legislation Greek citizens were categorized into *ethnikofrones* ('healthy, nationally-minded citizens') and the *non-ethnikofrones* (i.e. the communists, fellow-travellers and sympathizers. This legislation enabled the gendarmerie and the police to terrorize and persecute citizens of 'doubtful' political morality. See David H. Close, 'The Legacy' in David H. Close (ed.), *The Greek Civil War, 1943–1950: Studies of Polarization* (London: Routledge, 1993).
7. Tsigaridas court testimony, 21 October 2009. This deep ideological division between *ethnikofrones* and *non-ethnikofrones* lasted until 1974 with the transition to a democratic constitutional order and was to have serious side-effects on the evolution of Greek political culture in which extreme-left terrorism later developed.
8. Ibid.
9. Ibid.
10. Ibid.
11. Ibid.
12. EDA was, in effect, assigned by KKE's leadership in exile the task of advancing the Greek communist movement and thus preparing the ideological ground for the KKE leaders. The majority of EDA leaders were communists and among them a group called 'interior office' of the central committee was in charge of executing KKE's policies.
13. Tsigaridas court testimony, 21 October 2009.
14. See Panayotis Noutsos, *I Sosialistiki Skepssi stin Ellada: 1875–1974* [Socialist Thought in Greece: from 1875 to 1974] (Athens: Gnossi, 1994).
15. Tsigaridas court testimony, 21 October 2009.
16. Ibid.
17. Ibid. Andreas Papandreou, who Tsigaridas mentions, went a step further at the time calling *metapolitefsi* 'a change of guard'.
18. Ibid.
19. See Lina Alexiou, 'Katharsi-Apochountopoiissi-Ekdimokratismos: Chamenes Elpides, Olethries Parachorisseis' [Catharsis-Dejuntification-Democratization: Lost Opportunities, Calamitous Confessions] in *Anti* (No. 24, 1975); see also *Anti* editorials (No. 12, 1974); (Nos. 44,61, 1976); (Nos, 63, 65, 73, 86, 1977).
20. Tsigaridas court testimony, 21 October 2009.
21. Ibid.
22. Ibid.
23. Ibid.

24. Ibid.
25. Tsigaridas said he first met Kassimis by accident at the of 1975, early 1976 at a building site where he was working as an engineer. 'I saw Kassimis and realized that he and I went to same action committee even though he had not made an impression on me as he was not the type of person who would use verbal dexterity to capture an audience's imagination.'
26. Tsigaridas court testimony, 21 October 2009.
27. Ibid.
28. Ibid.
29. When Kassimis died, a replacement contact became automatically available.
30. Tsigaridas court testimony, 21 October 2009.
31. ELA manifesto 'Yia tin anaptyxi tou epanastatikou kai laikou kinimatos'.
32. Tsigaridas court testimony, 21 October 2009.
33. Ibid.
34. Ibid.
35. Ibid.
36. Ibid.
37. Ibid.
38. Ibid.
39. Ibid.
40. Ibid.
41. Ibid.
42. Ibid. The two stage theory (or stagism), approved also by the Greek communist party, which ELA attacked at every opportunity for 'poorly serving the working class' and 'making a valuable contribution to the consolidation of the bourgeois social order', was the Stalinist political theory which argues that underdeveloped countries, such as Tsarist Russia, had first to pass through a stage of bourgeois democracy before moving to a socialist stage.
43. See interview with Red Brigades dissosiatti Adriana Faranda, in Alison Jamieson's *The Heart Attacked: Terrorism and Conflict in the Italian State* (New York: Marion Boyars, 1989), p. 271.
44. Tsigaridas court testimony, 21 October 2009.
45. Ibid.
46. ELA manifesto 'Yia tin anaptyxi tou epanastatikou kai laikou kinimatos'.
47. Tsigaridas court testimony, 21 October 2009.
48. Tsigaridas court testimony, 21 October 2009.
49. Ibid.
50. Ibid.
51. Ibid.
52. Ibid.
53. Tsigaridas does make a valid point here as a total of 952 million euros annually, equivalent to 18.6 per cent of the Greek family budget or 20.1 per cent of the state budget for education, was spent by households in Greece in 2010 on particular courses and schools, according to a survey of European service NESSE.

54. Ibid. Serifis, who was a factory worker and a high-profile unionist at AEG, where ELA founder Christos Kassimis died, had to spend fifteen months in temporary custody before he was cleared by a Greek court in December 2003 of any involvement in the 17N group. Serifis had his first run-in with the law in 1977, when he was accused of taking part in a terrorist attack on a German company. The attack had ended in a shootout with police and the death of the first identified Greek terrorist, Christos Kassimis. Serifis was charged with murdering Kassimis, presumably to prevent him from falling into the hands of the police. He was acquitted of the charge two years later. When called to testify in the ELA trial, Serifis presented the magistrate with a written statement, in which he refused to testify or answer questions regarding his alleged involvement in a 1994 ELA bomb attack against a riot police bus. The invitation to testify 'offends me as citizen', he said.
55. 'Social change is possible because it historically necessary', Tsigaridas said in an interview to *Eleftherotypia* newspaper. 'And for that I am totally convinced ever since I first came to contact with Marxism and the communist movement at the age of eighteen.' *Eleftherotypia*, 11 October 2004.
56. See Robert Service, *Trotsky: A Biography* (London: Macmillan, 2009), p. 6.
57. Tsigaridas court testimony, 21 October 2009.
58. Tsigaridas court testimony, 21 October 2009; See also Tsigaridas's interview in *Eleftherotypia*, 11 October 2004.
59. Ted Robert Gurr, *Why Men Rebel*, (New Jersey: Princeton University Press, 1970) p. 211.
60. Tsigaridas court testimony, 21 October 2009.
61. Ibid.
62. *Eleftherotypia*, 11 October 2004. 'There have also been former fighters', Tsigaridas said in the same interview, 'who made sure with their behaviour afterwards to give themselves literally the characterization of former. Because, to take an example, if a fighter who was fighting against exploitation becomes an exploiter himself, he has without a doubt cancelled out his revolutionary consciousness and stained at the same time his own history. The same applies to a former revolutionary communist who now gives oaths of loyalty to parliamentary democracy.'
63. Ibid.
64. Tsigaridas court testimony, 21 October 2009.
65. Ibid.
66. Ibid.

6. GREECE'S NEW GENERATION OF TERRORISTS: THE REVOLUTIONARY STRUGGLE (RS)

1. 'New World Order or the Terrorism International' RS communiqué published in *To Pontiki*, 13 May 2004.
2. Ibid.

3. Ibid.
4. Ibid.
5. Ibid.
6. Ibid.
7. Ibid.
8. Ibid.
9. RS attack communiqué on George Voulgarakis,
10. Ibid.
11. Ibid.
12. Ibid.
13. RS communiqué on the US embassy in Athens, reprinted in *To Pontiki*, dated 25 January 2007.
14. Ibid.
15. Ibid.
16. Ibid.
17. Ibid.
18. Ibid.
19. On the Kaltezas incident see George Kassimeris, *Europe's Last Red Terrorists: The Revolutionary Organization 17 November* (London: Hurst, 2001), p. 79.
20. 'We Respond to Bullets with Bullets' RS communiqué, dated January 2009.
21. Ibid.
22. Ibid.
23. Ibid.
24. Ibid. Mirroring 17N's practice in describing the attack in great detail, RS presents a picture of a daring, audacious group of revolutionaries against a group of cowardly, incompetent and scared policemen. 'We decided', RS claimed in their 'We Respond to Bullets with Bullets' communiqué, 'to come face to face with the uniformed bullies of the regime, prepared even to engage with them with weapons and do battle. Two of us comrades went out on foot, walking slowly. We stopped at the junction of Koundouriotou and Notara streets. Exactly opposite were the three armed policemen who were monitoring the area at the rear of the Culture Ministry. They were not patrolling as it was said but were stationary. When we came around the corner, we stood in the middle of the road and turned our weapons against them without taking cover from anything, neither wall nor car. All three cops saw us immediately and all that was heard when they saw our weapons was an 'Oh' and nothing more. None of them warned anyone and they all three stood there watching us. While they had the opportunity to respond, they did not. After we started firing, the one on the right corner immediately took cover behind a car and did nothing to defend his two colleagues, even at a time when his position allowed him to use his weapon in safety. The second one fell flat in time and the third one fell down injured. A few meters away on Boumboulinas and Koundouriotou streets, there was a police bus full of MAT officers. There were almost twenty cops in and around the bus, who as well as

their own personal weapons also had automatics. None of them came out to the corner to respond and to defend their colleagues. We assume they must have fallen to the bus floor in order to save their skins. A valuable conclusion that does not have only military but also political implications is that when the regime's armed guards are faced with armed, determined revolutionaries, the "well-trained" dogs of the security forces, are merely armed "chickens" who dropped their shields and turned tail to hide.'

25. Ibid.
26. Ibid.
27. Ibid.
28. RS warned of the explosion by telephoning a newspaper, enabling the police to seal off the area before the bomb went off.
29. Athens Stock Exchange attack communiqué, undated.
30. Ibid.
31. Ibid.
32. Ibid.
33. Ibid.
34. Athens Court Archive, dated March 1999.
35. Ibid.
36. Ibid.
37. Ibid.
38. Interview, Athens, 15 February 2010.
39. RS attack communiqué on Citibank, dated 12 March 2009.
40. Ibid.
41. Interviews, Athens, June 2005.
42. See Timeline of RS attacks at the end of the chapter.
43. Interview, Athens, 25 April 2010.
44. Interview, Athens, 26 April 2010.

7. GREECE'S NEW GENERATION OF TERRORISTS, PART 2: THE CONSPIRACY OF CELLS OF FIRE (CCF)

1. In 2008, targets included the political office of the Minister of National Defence, Vaggelis Meimarakis, the military courthouse at Rouf, the French Press Agency, ACE Hellas Digital Systems, navy vehicles at the building entrance of Navy Command Headquarters, Klathmomos Square, Proton, Citybank, Millenium Bank, Eurobank, Geniki, Cyprus Bank, Agrotiki and Marfin Bank branches, the political office of the former Justice Minister Anastassis Papaligouras in Kolonaki, Porsche, Hyundai, Citroen and PV motors car dealerships, Greco-Italian School, Intersport, Goody's fast foods in Athens and Salonica, a Vodafone branch, New Democracy offices at Diikitirio, Salonica, diplomatic vehicles of the Czech Republic, Morocco and Italy, Interamerican Insurance and the club of reserve officers of the Greek armed forces in Evosmos, Salonica.

2. CCF communiqué dated 22 January 2008.
3. CCF communiqué posted on 21 March 2008.
4. On the night of 6 December at about 9 p.m., Epaminondas Korkoneas, a special guard seconded to the police, got out of his patrol car in Exarcheia, a rundown central district of Athens known as the home base of anarchists and extreme left-wingers, to confront a group of youths shouting abuse at him and his partner. Soon after the shooting of Grigoropoulos, police tried in vain to seal the area as hundreds of people had taken to the nearby streets to spread the news about the incident and express their anger against police brutality. A group of anarchists occupied the main building of the Athens Polytechnic and another group of militants the law faculty to use it as a centre of struggle. The clashes between police and protesters in the Exarcheia area lasted the rest of the night and the whole Sunday. By Monday lunch-time, thousands of students, pupils and citizens were out on the streets protesting against the police.
5. CCF communiqué posted on 21 March 2008.
6. CCF attack communiqué posted on 15 February 2009.
7. Ibid.
8. The extract was placed at the beginning of the communiqué starting with the verse 'this is the dead land/ this is cactus land'.
9. CCF attack communiqué posted on 12 January 2010.
10. Ibid.
11. Ibid.
12. Ibid.
13. Ibid.
14. Ibid.
15. Ibid.
16. This was the second communiqué in which CCF made a point of mentioning 17N's chief of operations. The group also paid tribute to urban guerrillas Christos Kassimis, Michalis Prekas, Christoforos Marinos, Christos Tsoutsouvis and Charis Tampakidis, 'who had lost their lives in their fight against the system for dignity and freedom'.
17. The house in Halandri had been monitored for months according to Greek counter-terrorism sources. More specifically, counterterrorism police had been monitoring suspects and several houses in anticipation of a politically motivated attack ahead of the 4 October national elections. The raid took place a day after a blast outside the home of Louka Katseli, PA.SO.K.'s Shadow Minister for Finance. The bomb, which was placed outside the apartment block where Katseli lives in Kolonaki, central Athens, was described by police as being 'of moderate strength'. It had been deposited in a cooking pot and planted outside the apartment, which is located on heavily policed Tsakalov Street. The cooking pot technique was used in July by Conspiracy of the Cells of Fire to target the home of former Deputy Interior Minister Panayiotis Hinofotis in Palaio Faliro.
18. C. Chatzimichelakis, E. Yiospas, P. Masouras and M. Panteloglou. The first three were remanded while Panteloglou was set free.

19. CCF Greek Parliament attack communiqué posted on 12 January 2010.
20. See *The Financial Times*, 3 November 2010.
21. 'Announcement Regarding our Arrested Comrades' communiqué dated 25 November 2010.
22. See Alison Jamieson, 'Entry, Discipline and Exit in the Italian Red Brigades' in *Terrorism and Political Violence*, Vol. 2 No. 1 (Spring 1990), pp. 1–20; and Dennis Pluchinsky 'An Organizational and Operational Analysis of Germany's Red Army Faction Terrorist Group (1972–91)' in Yonah Alexander and Dennis Pluchinsky (eds) *European Terrorism: Today & Tomorrow* (McLean, VA: Brassey's, 1992), pp. 43–79.
23. 'Announcement Regarding our Arrested Comrades' communiqué dated 25 November 2010.
24. Ibid.
25. Ibid.
26. Ibid.
27. Ibid.
28. Ibid.
29. Ibid.
30. Ibid.
31. Ibid.
32. Ibid.
33. Ibid.
34. Ibid.
35. Ibid.
36. Ibid.
37. Ibid.
38. Ibid.
39. Ibid.
40. Ibid.
41. According to police sources, a local resident had seen two men dressed in police uniforms pull up near the court building on the motorcycle in question at around 6:30 a.m. The witness actually spoke to them and they told him that they were abandoning the bike as it had developed engine problems. The pair then got into a white van parked nearby and were driven away by a third suspect.
42. Horst Fantazzini was an Italian anarchist, writer, and outlaw who used to rob banks with toy guns. He spent most of his life in and out of jail and died in December 2001 in Bologna prison after his last escape attempt. He was the son of the anarchist Libero Fantazzini.
43. The attack came three days after an Italian guerrilla group, called F.A.I or Federazione Anarchica Informale, claimed responsibility for a letter bomb that exploded at the Greek Embassy in Rome, injuring two people. FAI had also said in its communiqué that the attack had been staged to express solidarity with the CCF prisoners.

44. Administrative court attack communiqué, 5 January 2011.
45. Ibid.
46. Ibid.
47. Ibid.
48. Ibid.
49. Ibid. Towards the end of the communiqué CCF offered an operational description of the attack. The group said it was important to talk about some of their operations in order to demystify them. CCF believed that with good organization anything was operationally possible. On the operation itself the group said: 'We mapped out the area, we calculated the distance to the General Hospital so that not the slightest thing would go wrong, watched the movements and shifts of the special guard post between the administrative court and the appellate court, timed the blackout at 7:15 in the morning when the streetlights go out and the frequency of the DIAS [motorcycle police group] pigs around the target, we expropriated the vehicles we needed and went on the attack…We formed a fully operational team more than ready to attack in the event of any police involvement. Two support vehicles oversaw the court area before the planting of the bomb and at the final stage of its parking. The positioning of the support team was such that they would be able to immediately subdue the guard, had he realized anything but also to surprise any accidentally passing police car or motorbike. Our position and weapon superiority made disengagement straightforward.'
50. Ibid.
51. Koufodinas is expected to stay behind bars for at least twenty-five years.
52. See for instance interview with RAF imprisoned militants: 'Interview with four women political prisoners in Lübeck, Germany' in http://www.germanguerilla.com/red-army-faction/pdf/lubeck_interview.pdf
53. See 'Announcement Regarding our Arrested Comrades' communiqué dated 25 November 2010.
54. See letter from prison entitled 'A Small Contribution of the Imprisoned Members of the CCF about Solidarity', dated 4 May 2011. The letter was signed by Olga Oikonomidou, Panagiotis Argyrou, Charis Chadjimichelakis, Giorgos Nikolopoulos, Giorgos Polydoros, Christos Tsakalos, Gerasimos Tsakalos, Damianos Bolano and Michalis Nicholopoulos.
55. Undated letter entitled 'We have rage' by Gerasimos Tsakalos from Korydallos maximum security prison.
56. Ibid.
57. Ibid.
58. Ibid.
59. Ibid.
60. Ibid.
61. Ibid.
62. A female and two male employees of a Marfin bank branch died of asphyxiation after protesters broke the windows of a commercial building on Stadiou Avenue, in central Athens and tossed in Molotov cocktails.

63. Ibid.
64. Ibid.
65. Announcement of the defendants in the case of the R.O. Conspiracy of Cells of Fire, dated 3 February 2011.
66. Ibid.
67. Ibid.
68. Announcement of ending the hunger strike of the four defendants of the R.O. Conspiracy of Cells of Fire, dated 11 February 2011.
69. Ibid.
70. Ibid.
71. Ibid.
72. Ibid.
73. Karakatsani claimed in fact that the fingerprints that were found in the Halandri house were there because she was doing all the domestic jobs at the house.
74. Letter from Konstantina Karakatsani to *Eleftherotypia* dated 12 November 2009.
75. Ibid.
76. Ibid.
77. Ibid.
78. Letter from Konstantina Karakatsani from Korydallos prison, dated 25 February 2011.
79. Ibid.
80. Ibid.
81. Ibid.
82. Ibid.
83. Ibid.
84. Ibid.
85. Konstantina Karakatsani letter from Korydallos prison, dated 25 February 2011.
86. Posted on athensindymedia.org, 25 June 2011. See also *To Vima* of 23 January 2001, where the parents of five arrested members of CCF talk about their children and the possible reasons behind their engagement with terrorist violence. In April 2012, an appeals court panel approved Konstantina Karakatsani's conditional release.
87. Michael Dartnell makes a very interesting point about revolutionary violence and Nechaev in his *Action Directe: Ultra-left Terrorism in France, 1979–1987* (London: Frank Cass, 1995), p. 127.
88. This succession mechanism model was first introduced by the German RAF back in the 1980s: when a hard-core, or commando member was arrested or withdrew someone from the support level moved in as a replacement
89. Second period of CCF communiqué, posted 27 July 2011.

8. CONCLUSION

1. Joseba Zulaika, *Terrorism: The Self-Fulfilling Prophecy*, (Chicago: Chicago University Press, 2009), p. 10.

2. See Country Survey: Greece in *The Economist*, 10 October 2002.
3. The trial of ELA started two months after the end of the 17N trial, in February 2004.
4. See '17N: I diki den edose apantisseis' [The 17 trial did not give answers], *Kyriakatiki Eleftherotypia*, 30 November 2003.
5. For the 17N trial, the so-called 'Trial of the Century', six months after the draconian sentences were handed down the court produced a 6,600-page document explaining the ruling in exhaustive detail. Described in the ruling as 'the toughest and most murderous of all [domestic] organizations', 17N was seen by the court as a mixture of former anti-junta resistance fighters and dogmatic leftists who saw Greece's post-1974 transition to democracy as a perverse continuation of the Colonels' dictatorship. 17N, according to the ruling, was founded in 1974 by 'Alexandros Giotopoulos, Nikos Papanastasiou and two other as yet unknown individuals, one of them being a pretty-looking, blonde woman named Anna'. The court found Giotopoulos to be the 'intellectual helmsman who conveyed the death orders' but it also expressed the conviction that 17N was 'run by an executive secretariat'. Addressing widespread legal and media criticism that the convictions of several of the accused were based on testimony by others charged as 17N members, the court said that the rule that 'a guilty person cannot make another person guilty' applied only in cases where a single accused individual offered incriminating testimony against another accused individual. 'The evidentiary limitation provided by the law', the ruling further explained, 'applies only where one testimony or confession is involved, and not that of more charged individuals.' At the same time, the ruling dismissed charges of torture voiced during the trial by convicted 17N members like Savvas Xiros and Vassilis Tzortzatos.
6. Author interview, Athens September 2010. On the 17N trial see Nikolaos Zairis, *Ta Paraleipomena apo ti Diki tis EO 17N* [Omissions from the EO 17N trial] (Kalymnos: Drosos editions, 2009); Costas Botopoulos, *I Diki tis Megalis Dikis* [The Trial of the Big Trial] (Athens: Nefeli, 2004); Michalis Dimitriou, *Enorkos sti Diki gia tin 17N* [Juror for the 17N trial] (Athens: Stafylidis editions, 2004).
7. See for example, Alessandro Orsini, *Anatomy of the Red Brigades: The Religious Mind-set of Modern Terrorists*, (Ithaca: Cornell University Press, 2011) p. 258.
8. Zulaika, *Terrorism: The Self-Fulfilling Prophecy*, p. 109.
9. See Donatella Della Porta, *Social Movements, Political Violence, and the State: A Comparative Analysis of Italy and Germany* (Cambridge: Cambridge University Press, 1995), p. 195.
10. C. Von Clausewitz, *On War* (Harmondsworth: Penguin, 1968), p. 104.
11. See David Moss 'Politics, Violence, Writing; The Rituals of "Armed Struggle" in Italy' in David Apter (ed.) *The Legitimization of Violence* (London: Macmillan, 1997), p. 85.
12. See RS attack communiqué, dated 12 March 2009.

13. See David Apter 'Political Violence in Analytical Perspective' in David Apter (ed.) *The Legitimization of Violence* (London: Macmillan, 1997), p. 18.
14. Richard English, *Terrorism: How to Respond* (Oxford: Oxford University Press, 2009), p. 74.
15. Donatella Della Porta, *Social Movements*, p. 19.
16. See Tom Parker, 'Fighting an Antaean Enemy: How Democratic States Unintentionally Sustain Terrorist Movements they Oppose' in *Terrorism and Political Violence* (Vol. 19, No. 2, 2007), p. 172.
17. Court proceedings, Korydallos prison chambers, 24 July 2003.
18. Ibid.
19. Tsigaridas court testimony, 21 October 2009.
20. In June 2012, Maziotis, together with his partner and RS comrade Panagiota Roupa, went missing in the middle of their trial. The couple—who have admitted they are members of the group—were arrested in April 2010 but were released from jail in October 2011 after spending the maximum eighteen months in pre-trail detention, a time during which they had claimed to be political prisoners. They had been ordered to appear at a police station in the central Athens area of Exarchia three times a month, but according to police authorities missed their 15 June and 1 July appointments and have not been seen since.
21. Maziotis interview in *To Vima* newspaper, 16 October 2011.
22. In a letter dated 18 July 2010 Maziotis explained in detail the reasons behind his decision to go on hunger strike and called his yet to be born baby son 'the youngest political prisoner of the Greek "democracy"'. 'The treatment reserved by the Greek state', he wrote, 'for the imprisoned revolutionaries and its political enemies is standard: vengeful actions, sadism, physical and psychological violence, disrespect toward human dignity, indifference for health, for bodily integrity, for human life itself. Because the security of the state and the regime, is above everything else—above life itself and above "human rights".'
23. Author interview, Athens, 14 June 2011.
24. Martha Crenshaw, 'Thoughts on Relating Terrorism to Historical Contexts' in Martha Crenshaw (ed.), *Terrorism in Context* (Pennsylvania: Penn State Press, 1995), p. 14.
25. See David Apter (ed.), *The Legitimization of Violence*, (London, Macmillan, 1997), p. 2.
26. Ibid., p. 7.
27. See, for example, Jennifer L. Merolla and Elizabeth J. Zechmeister, *Democracy at Risk: How Terrorist Attacks Affect the Public* (Chicago: Chicago University Press, 2009) pp. 195–199.
28. In 2009, for example, there were 450 security-related incidents recorded in Athens alone, significantly more than in each of the previous twenty years (Greek Criminal Intelligence Directorate, Sept. 2010).
29. See, for example, Spyros Economides and Vassilis Monastiriotis (eds), *The Return of Street Politics: Essays on the December Riots in Greece*, (London: The Hellenic Observatory, LSE, 2009).

30. See Nikos Konstandaras, 'Greece: chronic insecurity and despair—welcome to life in a broken state', *The Guardian*, 16 June 2012; see also Randall Fuller, 'Paralysis in Athens', *The New York Times*, 6 June 2012.
31. See *Guardian* editorial 'Greek elections: the replay deepens the divide, 17 June 2012; see also Thodoris Georgakopoulos, 'The rise of Golden Dawn is a sign of Greek lawlessness', *The Guardian*, 14 June 2012 and Kerin Hope, 'Greece grapples with shadow of Golden Dawn', *The Financial Times*, 21 September 2012.

BIBLIOGRAPHY

Abrahams, Max, 'What Terrorists Really Want: Terrorist Motives and Counterterrorism Strategy' in *International Security* (Vol. 32, No. 4 Spring, 2008), pp. 78–105.

Alonso, Rogelio, 'Why Do Terrorists Stop? Analyzing why ETA Members Abandon or Continue with Terrorism' in *Studies in Conflict & Terrorism* (Vol. 34, No. 9, 2011).

Alexander, Yonah and Dennis Pluchinsky (eds), *European Terrorism: Today & Tomorrow* (McLean, VA: Brassey's, 1992).

Apter, David (ed.), *The Legitimization of Violence* (London: Macmillan, 1997).

Apter, David (ed.), *Ideology and Discontent* (London: Collier Macmillan, 1964).

Art, Robert J. and Louise Richardson (eds), *Democracy and Counterterrorism: Lessons from the Past* (Washington, DC: United States Institute of Peace Press, 2007).

Aust, Stefan, *The Baader Meinhof Complex* (London: Bodley Head, 2008).

Bandura, Albert, 'Mechanisms of Moral Disengagement' in Reich, Walter (ed.), *Origins of Terrorism; Psychologies, Ideologies, Theologies, States of Mind* (Cambridge: Cambridge University Press, 1990), pp. 161–91.

Berman, Paul, *Terror and Liberalism* (New York: Norton, 2004).

Byman, Daniel, *The Five Front War: The Better Way to Fight Global Jihad* (London: Wiley, 2008).

Byman, Daniel, 'The Decision to Begin Talks with Terrorists: Lessons for Policymakers' in *Studies in Conflict & Terrorism* (Vol. 29, No. 5, 2006) pp. 403–14.

Bobbitt, Philip, *Terror and Consent: The Wars For the Twenty-First Century* (London: Allen Lane, 2008).

Bolt, Neville, *The Violent Image: Insurgent Propaganda and the New Revolutionaries* (London: Hurst, 2012).

Booth, Ken and Tim Dunne, *Terror In Our Time* (London: Routledge, 2012).

Botopoulos, Costas, *I Diki tis Megalis Dikis* [The Trial of the Big Trial] (Athens: Nefeli, 2004).

Bloom, Mia, *Bombshell: The Many Faces of Women Terrorists* (London: Hurst, 2011).
Burleigh, Michael, *Blood & Rage: A Cultural History of Terrorism* (London: Harper Press, 2008).
Bjiorgo, Tore and John Horgan (eds), *Leaving Terrorism Behind: Individual and collective disengagement* (London: Routledge, 2009).
Carr, Matthew, *Unknown Soldiers: How Terrorism Transformed the Modern World* (London: Profile, 2006).
Canter, David (ed.), *The Faces of Terrorism: Multidisciplinary Perspectives* (Oxford: Wiley-Blackwell, 2009).
Catanzaro, Raimondo (ed.), *The Red Brigades & Left-Wing Terrorism in Italy* (London: Pinter, 1991).
Collins, Eamon, *Killing Rage* (London: Granta, 1997).
Chaliand, Gerard and Arnaud Blin (eds), *The History of Terrorism: From Antiquity to Al Qaeda* (Berkeley, CA: University of California Press, 2007).
Clark, Robert, 'Patterns in the Lives of ETA Members' in *Terrorism and Political Violence* (Vol. 6, No. 3, 1983), pp. 423–454.
Cordes, Bonnie, 'Euroterrorists Talk about Themselves: A Look at the Literature' in P. Wilkinson & A.M. Stuart (eds), *Contemporary Research on Terrorism* (Aberdeen: Aberdeen University Press, 1987), pp. 318–36.
Close, David H., 'The Legacy' in David H. Close (ed.), *The Greek Civil War, 1943–1950: Studies of Polarization* (London: Routledge, 1993).
Crenshaw, Martha (ed.), *Terrorism in Context* (Pennsylvania: Penn State Press, 1995).
Crenshaw, Martha, 'How Terrorism Declines' in *Terrorism and Political Violence* (Vol. 3, No. 1, 1991), pp. 69–87.
Cronin Kurth, Audrey, *How Terrorism Ends: Understanding the Decline and Demise of Terrorist Campaign*, (Princeton, NJ: Princeton University Press, 2009).
Dartnell, Michael, *Action Directe: Ultra-left Terrorism in France, 1979–1987* (London: Frank Cass, 1995).
Davies, Mike, *Buda's Wagon: A Brief History of the Car Bomb* (London: Verso, 2007).
Drake, Richard, *The Aldo Moro Murder Case* (London: Harvard University Press, 1995).
Debray, Regis, *Revolution in the Revolution?* (London: Penguin, 1967).
Decker, Scott H. and Barrik Van Winkle, *Life in the Gang: Family, Friends and Violence* (Cambridge: Cambridge University Press, 1996).
Della Porta, Donatella, *Social Movements, Political Violence, and the State: A Comparative Analysis of Italy and Germany*, (Cambridge: Cambridge University Press, 1995).
De Graaf, Beatrice and Malkki Leena, 'Killing it Softly? Explaining the Early Demise of Left-Wing Terrorism in the Netherlands' in *Terrorism and Political Violence* (Vol. 22, No. 4, 2010) pp. 623–640.

Devji, Faisal, *The Terrorist in Search of Humanity: Militant Islam and Global Politics* (London: Hurst, 2008).
Dimitriou, Michalis, *Enorkos sti Diki gia tin 17N* [Juror for the 17N trial] (Athens: Stafylidis editions, 2004).
Economides, Spyros and Vassilis Monastiriotis (eds), *The Return of Street Politics? Essays on the December Riots in Greece* (London: The Hellenic Observatory, LSE, 2009).
Ebaugh, Helen Rose Fuchs, *Becoming an Ex: The Process of Role Exit* (Chicago: Chicago University Press, 1988).
English, Richard, *Terrorism: How to Respond* (Oxford: Oxford University Press, 2009).
English, Richard, *Armed Struggle: The History of the IRA* (London: Macmillan, 2003).
Evangellou, Giannis et al, *I Politiki Via einai pantote Fasistiki* [Political Violence is Always Fascistic] (Athens: Diapyron, 2010).
Franceschini, Alberto, *Mara Renato e Io, Storia dei fondatori delle BR* (Milano: Armando Mondatori Editore, 1988).
Franceschini, Alberto and Giovanni Fasanella, *Che cosa sono le BR: Le radici, la nascita, la storia, il presente. Chi erano veramente i brigatisti e perché continuano a uccidere. Una nuova testimonianza del fondatore delle Brigate rosse* (Roma: Rizzoli: 2004).
Frampton, Martyn, *The Return of the Militants: Violent Dissident Republicanism* (London: The International Centre For the Study of Radicalisation and Political Violence, 2010).
Florez-Morris, Mauricio, 'Why Some Colombian Guerrilla Members Stayed in the Movement Until Demobilization: A Micro-Sociological Case Study of Factors that Influences Members' Commitment to Three Former Rebel Organizations: M-19, EPL and CRS' in *Terrorism and Political Violence* (Vol. 22, No. 2, 2010) pp. 216–241.
Graebner, William, *Patty's Got a Gun: Patricia Hearst in 1970s America* (Chicago: Chicago University Press, 2008).
Geltzer, Joshua, *US Counter-Terrorism Strategy and al-Qaeda* (London: Routledge, 2010).
Gray, John, *Al Qaeda and What it Means to be Modern* (London: Faber & Faber, 2003).
Gupta, Dipak, *Understanding Terrorism and Political Violence: The Life Cycle of Birth, Growth, Transformation and Demise* (London: Routledge, 2008).
Gurr, Ted Robert, *Why Men Rebel* (Princeton, NJ: Princeton University Press, 1970).
Hamiliton, Carrie, *Women and ETA: The Gender Politics of Radical Basque Nationalism* (Manchester: Manchester University Press, 2007).
Hart, Peter, *Mick: The Real Michael Collins* (London: Macmillan, 2005).
Hobsbawm, Eric, *Globalisation, Democracy and Terrorism* (London: Little, Brown, 2007).

Hoffman, Bruce, *Inside Terrorism* (London: Victor Gollancz, 1998).
Horgan, John, *Walking Away from Terrorism* (London: Routledge, 2009).
Horgan, John, *The Psychology of Terrorism* (London: Routledge, 2005).
Jamieson, Alison, *The Heart Attacked* (London: Marion Boyars, 1990).
Jamieson, Alison, 'Identity and Morality in the Italian Red Brigades', in *Terrorism and Political Violence*, Vol. 2, No. 4 (Winter 1990), pp. 508–20.
Jamieson, Alison, 'Entry, Discipline and Exit in the Italian Red Brigades' in *Terrorism and Political Violence* (Vol. 2 N.1, 1990), pp. 1–20.
Jacobson, Michael, *Terrorist Dropouts: Learning from Those Who Have Left* (Washington: The Washington Institute, Policy Focus No. 101, 2010).
Jones, Seth G. and Martin C. Libicki, *How Terrorist Groups End: Lessons for Countering al Qaida* (Santa Monica, CA: Rand Corporation, 2008).
Kassimeris, George, *Europe's Last Red Terrorists*: The Revolutionary Organization 17 November (New York: New York University Press, 2001).
Kassimeris, George, 'Greece: Twenty Years of Political Violence' in *Terrorism and Political Violence*, Vol. 7, No. 2 (Winter 1995).
Kirby, Aiden, 'The London Bombers as "Self-Starters": A Case Study in Indigenous Radicalization and the Emergence of Autonomous Cliques' in *Studies in Conflict & Terrorism* (Vo.30, No. 5, 2007). pp. 415–28.
Kydd, Andrew H., and Barbara F. Walter, 'The Strategies of Terrorism' in *International Security* (Vol. 31, No. 1, 2006), pp. 49–80.
Kruijt, Dirk, *Guerrillas* (London: Zed Books, 2008).
Lopez-Alves, Fernando, 'Political Crises, Strategic Choices and Terrorism: The Rise and Fall of the Uruguayan Tupamaros' in *Terrorism and Political Violence* (Vol. 1. No. 2, 1989), pp. 202–41.
LoCicero, Alice and Samuel J. Sinclair, 'Terrorism and Terrorist Leaders: Insights from Developmental and Ecological Psychology' in *Studies in Conflict & Terrorism* (Vol. 31, No. 3, 2008), pp. 227–250.
Lygeros, Stavros, '17 Noemvri: I Parakmiaki fasi tou tromokratikou fainomenou' [17 November: The decadent phase of the terrorist phenomenon] in *Tetradia* (No. 47, Winter 2002–3), pp. 13–19.
Lygeros, Stavros, 'Ta Dekemvriana: Mia eksegerssi choris kalous tropous' [The December events: A Revolt with bad manners] in *Tetradia* (No. 55–56, Spring-Summer 2009), pp. 11–21.
Malkki, Leena, *How Terrorist Campaigns End: The Campaigns of the Rode Jeugh in the Netherlands and the Symbionese Liberation Army in the United States* (Helsinki: University of Helsinki Press, 2010).
Mazower, Mark, *Inside Hitler's Greece: The Experience of Occupation 1941–44* (New Haven: Yale University Press, 1995).
Merolla, Jennifer L. and Zechmeister, Elizabeth J, *Democracy at Risk: How Terrorist Attacks Affect the Public* (Chicago: Chicago University Press, 2009).
Moghadan, Assaf, 'Failure and Disengagement in Red Army Faction' in *Studies in Conflict & Terrorism* (Vol. 35, No 2, 2012).

Michael, George, 'The Ideological Evolution of Horst Mahler: The Far Left-Extreme Right Synthesis' in *Studies in Conflict & Terrorism* (Vol. 32, No. 4, 2009), pp. 346–366.

Molony, Ed, *Voices From the Grave: Two Men's War in Ireland* (London: Faber & Faber, 2010).

Moss, David, 'Analyzing Italian Political Violence as a Sequence of Communicative Acts: The Red Brigades, 1970–1982', in *Social Analysis*, No. 3 (May 1983).

Moss, David, 'The Gift of Repentance: a Maussian Perspective on Twenty Years of Pentimento in Italy' in *European Journal of Sociology* (Vol. 42, N.2, 2001).

Moroni, Primo, (ed.) *Le Parole la Lotta Armata* (Milano: Shake Edizioni,1999).

Neumann, Peter and Smith, M.L.R, *The Strategy of Terrorism: How it Works, and Why it Fails* (London: Routledge, 2006).

Neumann, Peter, *Old & New Terrorism: Late Modernity, Globalization and the Transformation of Political Violence* (London: Polity, 2009).

Negri, Antonio, *Books For Burning: Between Civil War and Democracy in 1970s Italy* (London: Verso, 2005).

Negri, Antonio, *Du retour: Abécédaire biopolitique* (Paris: Calmann-Lévy, 2002).

Nerantzis, Pavlos, 'Francesco Piccioni: I zoi mou stis Erithres Taksiarchies—an interview [Francesco Piccioni: My Life inside the Red Brigades—an interview] in *Tetradia* (No. 408, Winter 2003–4), pp. 23–39.

Newman, Saul, *The Politics of Postanarchism* (Edinburgh: Edinburgh University Press, 2011).

Noutsos, Panayotis, *I Sosialistiki Skepssi stin Ellada: 1875–1974* [The Socialist Thought in Greece: from 1875 to 1974] (Athens: Gnossi, 1994).

O'Boyle, Garrett, 'Theories of Justification and Political Violence: Examples from Four Groups' in *Terrorism and Political Violence*, Vol. 14, No. 2 (Summer 2002).

Orsini, Alessandro, *Anatomy of the Red Brigades: The Religious Mind-set of Modern Terrorists*, (Ithaca: Cornell University Press, 2011).

Panourgia, Neni, *Dangerous Citizens: The Greek Left and the Terror of the State* (New York: Fordham University Press, 2009).

Paret, Peter, (ed.), *Makers of Modern Strategy* (Oxford: Oxford University Press, 1986).

Parker, Tom, 'Fighting an Antaean Enemy: How Democratic States Unintentionally Sustain Terrorist Movements they Oppose' in *Terrorism and Political Violence* (Vol. 19, No. 2, 2007), p. 172.

Perry, Mark, *How to Lose the War on Terror* (London: Hurst, 2010).

Pluchinsky, Dennis, *Europe's Red Terrorists: The Fighting Communist Organizations* (London: Frank Cass, 1992).

Post, Jerrold, *The Mind of the Terrorist: The Psychology of Terrorism from the IRA to Al Qaeda* (Basingstoke: Palgrave, 2007).

Post, Jerold, Ehud Sprinzak and Laurita Denny, 'The Terrorists in Their Own Words: Interviews with Thirty-Five Incarcerated Middle Eastern Terrorists' in *Terrorism and Political Violence* (Vo.15, No. 1, 2003), pp. 171–184.

Rapoport, David (ed.), *Inside Terrorist Organizations* (London: Frank Cass, 2001).

Rees, Phil, *Dining with Terrorists: Meetings with the World's Most Wanted Militants* (London: Macmillan, 2005).

Richardson, Louise, *What Terrorists Want: Understanding the Terrorist Threat* (London: John Murray, 2006).

Rosencof, Mauricio & Eleuterio Fernandez Huidobro, *Imerologio Filakis* [*Memorias del Calabozo*] (Athens: Koukkida editions, 2009).

Roncagliolo, Santiago, *La Cuarta Espada: La historia de Abimael Guzmán y Sendero Luminoso*, (Madrid: Debate, 2007. Greek edition: Kastaniotis, 2010).

Sageman, Mark, *Understanding Terror Networks* (Philadelphia: University of Pennsylvania Press, 2004).

Sayigh, Yezid, *Armed Struggle and the Search for State: The Palestinian National Movement 1949–1993* (Oxford: Oxford University Press, 1997).

Service, Robert, *Trotsky: A Biography* (London: Macmillan, 2009).

Schwarznmantel, John (ed.), 'Special Issue: Democracy and Violence' in *Democratization* (Vol. 17, No. 2, 2010).

Schiller, Margrit, *Remembering the Armed Struggle: Life in Baader-Meinhof* (London: Zidane Press, 2009).

Shirlow, Peter (et al), *Abandoning Historical Conflict? Former Political Prisoners and Reconciliation in Northern Ireland* (Manchester: Manchester University Press, 2010).

Smelser, Neil J., *The Faces of Terrorism: Social and Psychological Dimensions* (Princeton, NJ: Princeton University Press, 2007).

Sunstein, Cass R., *Going to Extremes: How Like Minds Unite and Divide* (Oxford: Oxford University Press, 2009).

Tolmein, Oliver, *RAF—Das war fur uns Befreiung: Ein Gespräch mit Irmgard Möller über bewaffneten Kampf, Knast und die Linke* (Konkret Literatur Verlag 1996). Greek edition: ΚΨΜ, 2007.

Toros, Harmonie, 'Terrorists, Scholars and Ordinary People: Confronting Terrorism Studies with Field Experiences' in *Critical Studies on Terrorism* (Vol. 1, No. 2, 2008), pp. 279–92.

Thorup, Mikkel, 'The Anarchist and the Partisan—Two Types of Terror in the History of Irregular Warfare' in *Terrorism and Political Violence* (Vol. 20, No. 3, 2008), pp. 333–335.

Varon, Jeremy, *Bringing The War Home: The Weather Underground, the Red Army Faction and Revolutionary Violence in the Sixties and Seventies* (Berkeley, CA, University of California Press, 2007).

Von Stetten, Moritz, 'Recent Literature on the Red Army Faction in Germany: a Critical Overview' in *Critical Studies on Terrorism* (Vol. 2, N.3, 2009), pp. 546–55.

Vittori, Jodi 'All Struggles Must End: The Longevity of Terrorist Groups' in *Contemporary Security Policy* (Vo.30, No. 3, 2009) pp. 444–466.

Waldmann, Peter, 'How Terrorism Ceases: The Tupamaros in Uruguay' in *Studies in Conflict & Terrorism* (Vol. 34, No 9, 2011) pp. 717–731.

Xiros, Savvas, *I Mera Ekeini: 1560 Ores stin Entatiki. Mia Martyria gia to diko mas Guantanamo'* [On That Day: 1560 Hours in Intensive care. An Eyewitness Account of our Guantanamo] (Athens: Alicia Romero, 2006).
Zairis, Nikolaos, *Ta Paraleipomena apo ti Diki tis EO 17N* [Omissions from the EO 17N Trial] (Kalymnos: Drosos Editions, 2009).
Zulaika, Joseba, *Terrorism: The Self-Fulfilling Prophecy*, (Chicago: Chicago University Press, 2009).

INDEX